Reviews of Companion Book

Exceptionally well written, organized and presented, *The Constitution Needs a Good Party* ... is as insightfully thoughtful and thought-provoking as it is ultimately hopeful and inspiring. An especially timely and unreservedly recommended addition to community, college, and university library American Political Science collections and supplemental curriculum studies lists ... [Also recommended] for the personal reading lists of students, academia, social activists, political reformers, governmental policy makers, and non-specialist general readers with an interest in the subject ....

— *Midwest Book Review*

Most politicians of both major parties totally ignore the Constitution. Generation after generation of politicians has expanded federal powers at the expense of state government authority and individual liberty. Judges have allowed this usurpation of power to continue unchecked.

James Anthony argues that a new political party is needed, a party that consists of individuals who recognize that the Constitution gives the federal government limited powers.

Millions of Americans have awakened to what is going on in their country. Perhaps it is not too late to turn the ship of state around.

— Robert W. McGee, professor, PhDs in economics, ethics, political philosophy, politics, law (JD & PhD), and more

rCONSTITUTION PAPERS

rCONSTITUTION PAPERS

OFFSETTING POWERS SECURE OUR RIGHTS

JAMES ANTHONY

np
Neuwoehner Press
St. Peters

Copyrighted Material

rConstitution Papers: Offsetting Powers Secure Our Rights

Copyright © 2020 by James Anthony. All Rights Reserved.

No part of this publication may be reproduced, stored in a retrieval system or transmitted, in any form or by any means—electronic, mechanical, photocopying, recording or otherwise—without prior written permission from the publisher, except for inclusion of brief quotations in a review.

For information about this title or to order other books and/or electronic media, contact the publisher:
Neuwoehner Press
28 Ellington Oaks Ct.
St. Peters, MO 63376

Library of Congress Control Number: 2019900710

ISBNs: 978-1-948177-04-7 (Hardcover)
978-1-948177-05-4 (Trade paperback)
978-1-948177-06-1 (EPUB e-book)
978-1-948177-07-8 (Kindle e-book)

Printed in the United States of America

Publisher's Cataloging-In-Publication Data

Names: Anthony, James, 1959– author.
Title: rConstitution papers : offsetting powers secure our rights / James Anthony.
Description: St. Peters, MO : Neuwoehner Press, [2020] | Includes bibliographical references and index.
Identifiers: ISBN 9781948177047 (hardcover) | ISBN 9781948177054 (trade paperback) | ISBN 9781948177061 (EPUB e-book) | ISBN 9781948177078 (Kindle e-book)
Subjects: LCSH: Political parties--United States. | United States--Politics and government. | Constitutional law--United States. | Separation of powers--United States. | Oaths--United States.
Classification: LCC JK2265 .A582 2020 (print) | LCC JK2265 (ebook) | DDC 324.273--dc23

Contents

rConstitution Paper 1:
  Good Government Comes from
  Good Boundaries 1.1
    Boundaries to Limit Government People . . . 1.2
    Government People Created
    the Financial Crisis of 2007 . . . . 1.4
    Good Boundaries Secure Freedom 1.8
    Bad Boundaries Caused the Crisis 1.11
    Knowledge Is Power 1.13

rConstitution Paper 2:
  Washington, Reagan, and Everyone Else 2.1
    Washington's Road to 100% Electoral Win . . 2.3
    Reagan's Road to 91% Electoral Win 2.7
    Voters Just Need the Choice 2.9

rConstitution Papers: Offsetting Powers Secure Our Rights

rConstitution Paper 3:
Individual Rights Are Secured
When Constitutional Powers Are Used 3.1
   Simple Scope, Simple Processes 3.2
   Securing Boundaries 3.8
   Using Offsetting Powers 3.14
   Securing Life, Liberty, and Property 3.15

rConstitution Paper 4:
Laws That Aren't Readable
Aren't Constitutional 4.1
   A Man's Got to Know His Limitations 4.2
   Nothing Exceeds like Excess 4.6
   Multiple Layers of Protection 4.8
   Stop Fueling the Fire 4.10

rConstitution Paper 5:
Laws That Direct the Executive or Direct
the Judiciary Are Unconstitutional 5.1
   Don't Grab Executive Power 5.2
   Don't Grab Judicial Power 5.6
   Simple Rules for a Complex World 5.8

rConstitution Paper 6:
Laws That Delegate Legislative Authority
Are Unconstitutional 6.1
   The Fountainhead Is Laws 6.2

Contents

> Blank Checks to Coerce 6.4
> Back Scratch Fever 6.8
> Constitutional Remedies 6.10

rConstitution Paper 7:
Laws That Mislead Are Unconstitutional . . . 7.1
> If Government Was Small 7.1
> When Laws Mislead 7.6
> Property Is Destroyed 7.12

rConstitution Paper 8:
Laws That Exceed Enumerated Powers
Are Unconstitutional 8.1
> Political, Commercial, and Support Scope . . 8.4
> False Rationalizations 8.5
> USA Created to End Scope Creep 8.7

rConstitution Paper 9:
Abortion Is Illegal 9.1
> Unborn Babies Are Alive 9.2
> Simultaneous Contraception
> Prevents Conception 9.4
> An Abortion Comes after Many Choices . . . 9.8
> Rights Are Mostly Secured by Structure . . 9.14
> Liberty Needed Support 9.16
> Life Needs Support 9.19
> Life Will Win Out in the End 9.25

ix

rConstitution Papers: Offsetting Powers Secure Our Rights

rConstitution Paper 10:
Fractional-Reserve Banking
Is Unconstitutional 10.1

   Good Money Matters 10.2

   GME "Gimme" Government Money
Error Cycles per Austrian Economics 10.5

   Lossy Money Stock 10.10

   Constant Money Stock 10.16

   Productive Money Stock 10.20

rConstitution Paper 11:
Laws Authorizing Military Action
Are Unconstitutional 11.1

   Resistance and Strength 11.1

   Inadequate Resistance, and Government
Destruction of Economic Strength 11.4

   Changing the Things That Are
within Your Control. 11.8

   Moral War 11.11

   Peacemaking Boundaries in the
Constitution 11.14

rConstitution Paper 12:
Block Grants Are Unconstitutional 12.1

   Block Grants Are Big Government 12.1

   Government Spending Is the Worst 12.4

   Free Cooperation Is Best 12.6

Contents

Coercion by State-Government People . . . 12.10

Coercion by National-Government
People Too. 12.13

In Governments, Least Is Best 12.14

rConstitution Paper 13:
Filibuster/Cloture Is Unconstitutional 13.1

Simple-Majority Voting
Is Plainly Required 13.1

Simple-Majority Voting Is Always Best . . . 13.5

rConstitution Paper 14:
Unadvised and Unconsented Treaties
Are Unconstitutional 14.1

Treaties Are Law 14.1

Laws Are Limited. 14.2

Presidents Aren't Lawmakers 14.3

Unilateral Actions Are Strong 14.5

Treaties Can Be Jumpstarts 14.13

Constitutional Senators Needed 14.17

rConstitution Paper 15:
NATO Is a Sham. 15.1

Moral War Must Follow the Constitution . . 15.1

Forward Basing Doesn't Follow
the Constitution. 15.4

xi

War Treaties Don't Follow
the Constitution. 15.6

War Treaties Create Immoral Wars 15.8

NATO Creates Immoral Wars. 15.10

rConstitution Paper 16:
Failure to Impeach and Convict
Denies People Their Rights. 16.1

Preventing Losses 16.2

Limiting Losses 16.4

Using Offsetting Powers 16.6

Using Impeachment 16.10

Zero Tolerance 16.16

Progressives Don't Represent Us 16.23

rConstitution Paper 17:
Congressional Oversight
Is Constitution Defiance 17.1

Defiance on War 17.1

Defiance on Agencies. 17.6

Progressives in Both Parties 17.15

rConstitution Paper 18:
Nominating Rules for Brand Purity. 18.1

The First Republicans 18.1

Democrats at First 18.3

Republicans 18.5

Contents

Democrats Postwar 18.6
Crisis and Leviathan 18.8
The Constitution for Crisis Prevention . . . 18.10
A New Party Design 18.14
Only a Party Has Enough Control Power . . 18.18

References R1.1

Index I.1

Figures

Figure 4.1:
Agency restrictions have built up
considerably and have kept trending up . . . 4.11

Figure 10.1:
Total real returns on USA stocks,
government long-term bonds, government
short-term Treasury bills, gold, and
dollars, 1802–2012 . . . . 10.21

Figure 12.1:
Free customers drive efficiency and
innovation. 12.6

Figure 13.1:
After the Berlin Wall was torn down,
fast change brought good results fast,
and the progress kept up 13.6

Tables

Table 2.1:
First-time electoral vote percentages of presidents who rose to office by electoral wins 2.2

Table 3.1:
Constitutional scope 3.4

Table 3.2:
Constitutional processes 3.6

Table 3.3:
Offsetting powers in Constitution 3.14

Table 8.1:
Constitutional scope 8.2

Table 11.1:
World War II GDP ratios and correlates 11.5

Table 11.2:
Rules of Engagement (ROE) card given
theatre-wide warning 11.19

Table 16.1:
Offsetting powers in Constitution 16.7

rConstitution Paper 1

Good Government Comes from Good Boundaries

GOOD BOUNDARIES, like good fences, make good neighbors.

Some important personal boundaries come into existence very naturally. A dog starts barking as soon as we walk into his family's property, and stops barking as soon as we walk out of his family's property.[1.1] A 3-year-old protests if the play-dough object she fashioned starts to be taken away by someone who wants it for himself.[1.2]

Securing such boundaries doesn't come about as naturally. If a boundary protects your space, then the boundary stops others from getting what they want from you, when they want it. So sometimes people cross your boundaries.

Securing your boundaries requires you to speak up in a way that protects your space without stepping into someone else's space and telling them what to do. It requires you to really listen to their pushback. It requires you to speak up again, once again respecting both your boundaries and theirs, and really listen again. It requires you to keep this up until the other person really listens to you too.[1.3]

Boundaries to Limit Government People

Securing boundaries is uniquely difficult when an aggressor has the force of a government on his side. This was the problem faced by the Founding Fathers who fought a war to secure their people's individual liberty from King George III. They won that war, but they still needed to secure their people's individual liberty using some new form of government that had never been tried before.

The boundaries that they brought into existence separated the people who wrote laws, the people who executed laws, and the people who judged cases. Such boundaries had been suggested before in theory, and had been partially tried out in practice, but had never before been made complete. Now, the Constitution of the

Good Boundaries

United States of America defined these boundaries clearly and completely. Articles I, II, and III respectively led with the statements that "All legislative Powers herein granted shall be vested in a Congress...," "The executive Power shall be vested in a President...," and "The judicial Power of the United States shall be vested in one supreme Court, and in such inferior Courts as the Congress may from time to time ordain and establish."

Securing these boundaries wasn't something that could be done just as clearly and completely. Here, the Founding Fathers devised a number of offsetting powers. But in the same way that securing personal boundaries requires that a person has the personal integrity, skill, and follow-through to speak out and to listen with care, securing government people's boundaries requires that other government people have the personal integrity, skill, and follow-through to exercise their powers. What could go wrong?

Well, there has been no problem with the Constitution, possible candidates, or voters. The Constitution defines a robust, multilayered set of offsetting powers. People who have good boundaries can be found in all walks of life. And when constitutionalist candidates like Washington and Reagan have made it onto ballots where voters could choose, voters have overwhelmingly preferred such candidates.

The root problem has been that neither the Founders nor their successors ended up also creating a party that has good boundaries separating the party people who write party laws, the party people who execute party laws, and the party people who judge party cases. All parties so far have lacked a good, resilient structure.

As a result, all parties so far have either begun in cronyism or fallen into cronyism. Since 1894[1.4] both major parties' people in government have not used their constitutional powers against others in government.

We can understand this problem, and we will solve this problem. As the Israeli politician and diplomat Abba Eban put it, "Men and nations behave wisely when they have exhausted all other resources."[1.5]

Government People Created the Financial Crisis of 2007

A number of ways that government people have failed to secure these constitutional boundaries will be evident in a single example that still personally affects everyone: the financial crisis of 2007. Here, we pick up the story earlier.

Good Boundaries

In 1938 the Federal National Mortgage Association or FNMA ("Fannie Mae") was created to borrow from the USA treasury and to loan to banks and savings & loans in order to finance mortgages. In 1954 the FNMA started selling common stock to private investors. In 1968 the FNMA's privately-owned operations were spun off by Congress and the president as a corporation called the FNMA.[1.6] In 1970 the Federal Home Loan Mortgage Corporation or FHLMC ("Freddie Mac") was created to also borrow from the USA treasury and to loan to banks and savings & loans in order to finance mortgages.[1.7]

The FNMA and the FHLMC are organized to give them many of the same features as traditional corporations, but they're not traditional corporations. In each of the two corporations, 5 of the 18 members of the board of directors are appointed by the USA president. Each corporation's share pricing can be propped up by the USA treasury secretary, who is preauthorized to buy up each corporation's securities in the amount of up to $2.25 billion. Each corporation is exempt from state and local taxes. Each corporation's charter limits its focus to buying up residential mortgages originated by others. And each corporation's charter requires it to strive to meet annual goals of the USA Department of Housing and Urban Development for ensuring that housing loans are made to people with lower incomes.[1.8]

In 1992 the goal became that the proportion of FNMA and FHLMC mortgages that were to people earning below the median income would be 30%. In 1995, 42%. In 2000, 50%. By 2008, 56%. Plus, by 2008 a second goal became that the proportion of FNMA and FHLMC mortgages that were to people earning 80% or less of the median income would be 27%. From 1996 through 2008, these goals were met almost every year.

Meanwhile, the USA Federal Housing Administration was already tasked with making loans to people with lower incomes.

Also, starting in 1994 the USA Department of Housing and Urban Development set up a Best Practice Initiative to make the members of the Mortgage Bankers Association reduce their requirements on borrowers' ability to repay mortgages.

Plus, starting in 1995 the Community Reinvestment Act required all insured banks and savings & loans to prove that they were making loans—including mortgages—to people earning 80% or less of the median income.

Good Boundaries

By 2008, the proportion of mortgages that were to people earning below the median income, or that had risky terms (adjustable rates, inadequate documentation, no principal repayments required, rental properties), was 49%.[1.9]

With this foundation in place, the stage was set for the timing of the financial crisis to be determined by more factors that were piled on.

Government people eliminated tax deductions for loans other than mortgages, so naturally people spent more money on mortgages.

Government people lowered interest rates, so naturally people spent even more money on mortgages.

Government people permitted overnight repurchase agreements. With these agreements, if lenders ever lose confidence and stop making the same agreement the next night, then borrowers need to immediately liquidate assets; but in a panic, buyers won't pay the full market value of the underlying assets. So given these agreements, naturally the borrowing financial institutions became vulnerable to runs on the "bank."

Government people mandated the use of mark-to-market accounting rules, so naturally financial institutions became worthless if no buyers were buying.

1.7

The net result was that government people increased home ownership in the short run, but not in the long run.

Home ownership isn't a leading indicator of how people will be doing in future years, it's a trailing indicator of how people have been doing in past years. To produce the real, lasting change that government people wanted the statistics to show, what government people would actually need to do is not what they actually did, but the exact opposite.

Government people would need to move to smaller government and exert minimal government control, which would make way for a larger private sector that would grow faster. This would let people earn more, would help people qualify as likely to pay off their mortgages, would help people buy homes, and would help people succeed at paying off their mortgages.

Good Boundaries Secure Freedom

The basics about the value of smaller government were well known by the people who developed the Constitution, from their personal experience. Back then, even people who were rich by the standards of the day were making their living through activities that were much nearer to subsistence-level than the way we live today.

James Madison, the author of the Constitution's key starting point, the Virginia Plan, ran a farm, distillery, and blacksmith shop.[1.10, 1.11] Gouverneur Morris, the author of the Constitution's preamble and also the final editor of the Constitution, practiced law and sold merchandise.[1.12]

With incomes much lower back then, taxes mattered a lot. New York, Massachusetts Bay, and Delaware were each established as tax havens. A century and a half later, compared to the tax rates of British citizens, the tax rates of New Englanders were only 1/20th or 1/10th as high.

Under tax burdens that were lower, growth was greater. By the time of the Revolution, the per-capita income purchasing power in America exceeded that in Great Britain by 68%.[1.13]

The problem with bigger government is that government people succeed by producing appearances—by appearing important and winning votes—not by adding value. Government people just need to earn votes every now and then, but people in business need to convince significant numbers of people to exchange some of their own hard labor for the business people's products on an ongoing basis.

This means that people in business have to add value all of the time. When they don't add value as well as other people in business add value, customers vote with their feet, every day. Groups of people in business who do better at adding value get stronger, and groups of people in business who do worse at adding value find that fairly soon they have to find new jobs with other people in business who will use their talents better and add more value. The most-fit organizations naturally get stronger over time, and the overall performance of people in business naturally improves over time.

Unfortunately, there's no such mechanism naturally strengthening the performance of people in government now. The reason a similar mechanism isn't at work in government is that apart from brief periods that were exceptions, both major parties have been enacting nearly the same policies since the onset of the Progressive Era more than a century ago. Voters don't get enough constitutionalist candidates to vote for in general elections to be able to vote higher-performing representatives into office.

The people who developed the Constitution understood the value of the boundaries that they were creating, and that they were creating powers to secure.

Bad Boundaries Caused the Crisis

In the run-up to the financial crisis of 2007 and to the Great Recession that followed, quite a few boundaries were not secured by quite a few of our government people.

Creation of and participation in the Federal National Mortgage Association and the Federal Home Loan Mortgage Corporation are not within the limited scope of the national government, which is established by the enumerated powers in USA Constitution Article I, Section 8. These enumerated powers define a boundary, a boundary that limits the national government's activities to addressing funding, citizenship, bankruptcy, federal government securities and currency, weights and measures, mail, copyrights and patents, national courts, international laws, wars, and the District of Columbia. The national government is not empowered to create corporations that compete with private corporations, to give special privileges to favored corporations, and to increase affordable housing.

This boundary is defined clearly in the Constitution. Securing this boundary are several independent powers. Failing to secure this boundary required multiple groups of people to independently fail to use these powers over an extended period of time.

When a Congress passed a bill unconstitutionally creating the FNMA or the FHLMC, the president could have vetoed the bill. The Supreme Court could have taken up a case and written a majority opinion that the law was unconstitutional.

Every Congress after that could have formally passed bills repealing the existing unconstitutional laws. Every president after that could have signed those bills into laws. In the meantime, every president after that also had all the national government's executive power, giving him the power to not execute any existing laws that in his opinion were unconstitutional. Every Supreme Court after that could have taken up a case and issued a majority opinion that the laws were unconstitutional.

The actions that these people actually took did not use the powers they were constitutionally entrusted with using. Instead, their actions took three forms: First, Congress people and presidents took the existing framework of unconstitutional laws, stretched them or added to them to temporarily increase home ownership, and spoke up to take credit for increasing home ownership. Second,

President George W. Bush wrote letters warning of problems; but just like the previous presidents, President Bush failed to use his constitutional powers to not execute the unconstitutional laws. Third, Supreme Courts didn't take up cases that challenged the unconstitutional laws.

Government people in each area of service, in each term of office, each of whom was individually empowered to secure the boundaries of the national government to protect individual liberty, drove right through all of those restraining orders.

The end result was that these ultimate too-big-to-fail corporations did fail. And individuals paid a high price: partly in higher taxes and partly in an overburdened, weak economy, which cost some people time out of work, and which cost all people either reductions in their standard of living or reduced gains in their standard of living.

Knowledge Is Power

The reason we have representatives who don't use their constitutional powers to secure the boundaries defined by the Constitution is that, for now, voters don't get enough constitutionalist candidates to vote for in general elections.

But knowledge is power. Plus, a great deal of what we need to know in this situation is information that we learned before we reached kindergarten, together with other information that we've learned informally in our lives by just living together with other people.

Good boundaries, in government people, limit government. This frees each person to create maximum added value, creating value that spills over and helps everyone. And this frees each person to more-fully live the way that he values the most.

rConstitution Paper 2

Washington, Reagan, and Everyone Else

OFTEN PEOPLE WEIGH IN about which candidate in a given primary race is the most-conservative candidate who can win. The better question is: What kind of candidate wins big?

The vote that decides presidential elections is the electoral vote. In all of history, the electoral vote has brought us new presidents 33 times. These electoral votes are listed in Table 2.1 below in order of the electoral vote percentages. These first-time electoral vote percentages exceeded 90% for just two presidents: George Washington and Ronald Reagan.

2.1

Table 2.1. *First-time electoral vote percentages of presidents who rose to office by electoral wins*[2.1]

President	Year	Votes	Total	%
George Washington	**1789**	**69**	**69**	**100%**
Ronald Reagan	**1980**	**489**	**538**	**91%**
Franklin Roosevelt	1932	472	531	89%
Franklin Pierce	**1852**	**254**	**296**	**86%**
James Monroe	**1816**	**183**	**217**	**84%**
Herbert Hoover	1928	444	531	84%
Dwight Eisenhower	1952	442	531	83%
Woodrow Wilson	1912	435	531	82%
William Harrison	**1840**	**234**	**294**	**80%**
George H. W. Bush	1988	426	538	79%
Warren Harding	**1920**	**404**	**531**	**76%**
Ulysses Grant	**1868**	**214**	**294**	**73%**
James Madison	**1808**	**122**	**175**	**70%**
Bill Clinton	1992	370	538	69%
Andrew Jackson	**1828**	**178**	**261**	**68%**
Barack Obama	2008	365	538	68%
William Taft	1908	321	483	66%
James Polk	**1844**	**170**	**275**	**62%**
William McKinley	**1896**	**271**	**447**	**61%**
Abraham Lincoln	**1860**	**180**	**303**	**59%**
James Buchanan	**1856**	**174**	**296**	**59%**
Benjamin Harrison	**1888**	**233**	**401**	**58%**
James Garfield	**1880**	**214**	**369**	**58%**
Martin Van Buren	**1836**	**170**	**294**	**58%**
Donald Trump	2016	304	538	57%
John Kennedy	1960	303	537	56%
Zachary Taylor	**1848**	**163**	**290**	**56%**
Richard Nixon	1968	301	538	56%
Jimmy Carter	1976	297	538	55%
Grover Cleveland	**1884**	**219**	**401**	**55%**
John Adams	**1796**	**71**	**138**	**51%**
George W. Bush	2000	271	538	50%
Rutherford Hayes	**1876**	**185**	**369**	**50%**

Constitutionalist
Progressive

Washington's Road to 100% Electoral Win

George Washington is described by historian John Ferling as one of the very-best politicians in American history.[2.2]

Washington had a modest inheritance. He lacked formal education,[2.3] but he read widely.[2.4] He took huge risks, financially and physically.[2.3]

Washington was an active businessman. He owned property and expanded his holdings. He managed his business and relatives' business. He diversified out of tobacco and into wheat, milling, horses, hogs, spinning, weaving, and distilling.[2.5]

In the French and Indian War and then again in the Revolutionary War, Washington at first bitterly opposed the strategy that in the end brought victory. Even so, he started with powerful benefactors, he built up staunch supporters, and he was a great leader. His character, judgment, prudence, and industriousness set him apart.[2.6]

As a representative in government, Washington lived in the wealthiest region by far,[2.7] lived in the colony that had the most land and the most people, and served in that colony's first legislature. After Great Britain passed the 1767 Townshend Acts on the American Colonies, Washington introduced George Mason's proposal to boycott British goods, and the acts were repealed in 1770. After Great Britain passed the 1774 Intolerable Acts on the American Colonies, Washington chaired a meeting that called for the convening of a Continental Congress, and he was elected to the Continental Congress.[2.5] In 1785, Washington and his neighbor George Mason resolved to have a partial Virginia delegation meet with a Maryland delegation to work out shared use of the Potomac River. They worked out this practical governance problem by meeting, the meeting became an annual event, and the annual event soon expanded to become the Constitutional Convention.[2.8] In 1787, Washington was unanimously elected the Constitutional Convention's president.[2.5]

Historian Edward Larson says that if James Madison was the Constitution's architect, then Washington was the Constitution's general contractor. Washington's 1783 circular letter was the country's best-known document other than the Declaration of Independence, so his presence at the Constitutional Convention was a strong vote in favor of a national government. Washington and James Madison were the only delegates who attended every session. Before a quorum arrived, the outlines of the design of the new government were cobbled together by the Virginians present and the Pennsylvanians. Washington met in small groups with various delegates in the evenings. Throughout, Washington modeled that a single person could be trusted as president. In the most-split delegation—that of Virginia—Washington cast the tie-breaking vote. Washington's signature was on the Constitution's cover letter and on accompanying resolutions calling for states to ratify the Constitution and to send electors and set a date for the new government to assume power. This made it look almost like the Constitution had been developed by Washington. And the Constitution, together with the Bill of Rights, was ratified.

In 1789, Washington was elected president unanimously. As president, he showed by example that the president, Congress, and the Supreme Court should each interpret the Constitution independently, and that each should back their independent interpretations by exercising the powers given them by the Constitution in the ways required by the independent interpretations that each is responsible for making.[2.9]

Throughout his life, Washington taught himself by reading, steadily learning what he needed at a given time to succeed. Early on, he read about military history and theory. When it became his job to raise the new Virginia Regiment, he read about tactics and organization of small units. Later he was managing multiple plantations, some of them unprofitable, and he read about agricultural science and learned what he needed to move away from unprofitable tobacco. As he started playing a role in politics, he read up on the controversies of the day. He read newspapers voraciously. During the Revolutionary War, he studied field manuals and learned to live within his side's limitations. He collaborated with media to help shape accounts of the American Revolution. He was among the first who suggested taking the ratification debate to the newspapers to build support for the Constitution.[2.10]

Thomas Jefferson and James Madison had key roles in writing the Declaration of Independence and the Constitution, but their political policies changed considerably in their lives; in contrast, Washington's political policy formed when he was young and remained largely the same from that point forward. Washington believed in individual liberty, secured against other world powers by a strong union,[2.11] with republican government, under the Constitution. And he poured his life and energy into bringing this constitutional government to life.

Reagan's Road to 91% Electoral Win

Ronald Reagan, like the Founders, had practical work experience and learned from it, and from this experience he came to believe strongly in following the Constitution, as explained by Reagan advisor Thomas Evans.[2.12]

Reagan's family worked hard to elect Franklin Roosevelt, and would gather as a family to listen to Roosevelt's warm fireside chats on the radio. Reagan was the spokesman for his fellow students at Eureka College who struck to reverse changes that would have kept them in college longer. He campaigned for Harry Truman, for Hubert Humphrey, and as a Democrat for Dwight Eisenhower. He called himself a "liberal Democrat" and a "New Dealer to the core."

Meanwhile, Reagan worked most of his adult life in business and business-related work. He worked as a radio sportscaster, an actor, a union leader, a spokesman for management, and a highly-sought speaker. The work as a management spokesman was for General Electric for 8 years. In these years Reagan gained a crucial civic education, and his beliefs shifted and matured significantly.

During Roosevelt's years, unions had gained political grants of monopoly power over workers.

After World War II, unions worked to monetize this power by threatening strikes and by striking to extract all possible rents from their host businesses. Given this anti-competitive surge, General Electric competed by innovating to go over the heads of union leaders and establish stronger relationships directly between managers and workers. Reagan joined this effort and became a visible and effective spokesman.

In this effort, GE published two weekly newsletters, a weekly newspaper, a quarterly journal, and manuals for managers. GE encouraged managers to read the Wall Street Journal editorial page, National Review, and Freeman Magazine. GE organized 16-week book clubs for employees and spouses, and often chose very-readable conservative economics books. GE employees who Reagan met around the country had lots of comments and questions about all this reading, and Reagan got himself prepared. As he traveled to all of the GE sites in 40 states—taking trains since he was afraid of flying—he read up.

Reagan got started reading when he was young, before he started in school, and he never let up. Right before he started at GE, he worked for two weeks as emcee at the Last Frontier Hotel in Las Vegas, and he and his wife Nancy carried in a "small library" of books. The owner had never seen an entertainer bring books to Las Vegas before. Reagan read slowly, remembering much of what he read, which helped him write many of his own speeches and answer questions off-the-cuff. By the time Reagan started prepping on local issues to run for governor, his library was stacked with books on political philosophy, and his philosophy was constitutional.

Sixteen years before he was elected president, Reagan took "The Speech" he had delivered so often on behalf of GE, and delivered it on behalf of presidential candidate Barry Goldwater. The speech was full of applications of moral and economic principles to current policy questions. But before getting into specifics, Reagan first stated clearly that "the full power of centralized government was the very thing the Founding Fathers sought to eliminate." Reagan understood and advocated strongly for the Constitution.

Voters Just Need the Choice

Supporters of unconstitutional centralized government have always been among us; even the founding generation's anti-Federalists worked presciently to fight this. But through much of our history, these supporters' impulses were considerably restrained by a shared understanding that such centralization was illegal.

Near the dawn of the 20th century this consensus was broken by the rise to power in both major parties of Progressives. The Constitution provides offsetting powers for different government people to use against one another to secure individual liberties from the growth of the national government, but this Progressive party duopoly enabled government people to collude to not use these offsetting powers, and to erect an increasingly unconstitutional national government.

Given that there was a step change in defiance of the Constitution when Progressives came to power, Table 2.1 defines constitutionalist presidents as those who were in office before the rise of the Progressives, plus later presidents who were comparatively faithful to the Constitution. The table also identifies presidents who were elected on the coattails of constitutionalist presidents.

Taken together, the constitutionalist presidents and their successors who promised to also be constitutionalist (Herbert Hoover and George H. W. Bush) totaled 22 of the 33 first-time electoral winners. The odds were 2 out of 3.

These are odds that a party can be built upon. And that's the party that voters need.

rConstitution Paper 3

Individual Rights Are Secured When Constitutional Powers Are Used

WE HOLD THESE TRUTHS *to be self-evident, that all men are created equal, that they are endowed by their Creator with certain unalienable Rights, that among these are Life, Liberty and the pursuit of Happiness.— That to secure these rights, Governments are instituted among Men, deriving their just powers from the consent of the governed* …[3.1]

The enumeration in the Constitution, of certain rights, shall not be construed to deny or disparage others retained by the people.[3.2]

The Declaration of Independence says that governments exist to secure people's God-given rights. The Constitution secures people's God-given rights not by listing all of these rights, but by governing the government people's scope and processes.

Simple Scope, Simple Processes

The scope defines a boundary, and the processes secure the boundary. A secure boundary works better for both parties involved. For the people outside a secure boundary that encloses the government, this boundary secures their God-given rights. For the government people working inside a secure boundary that encloses the government, this boundary gives them the maximum-permissible latitude to work out solutions that work well for the government people.

To hold government people accountable for securing this boundary, voters need to understand this boundary's defining scope and securing processes.

The full government scope permitted by the Constitution is summarized in Table 3.1 on pages 3.4 and 3.5, and the major ongoing processes are summarized in Table 3.2 on page 3.6.

When Powers Are Used

A quick look at these tables makes several structural features plain. The states *delegated* scope to the national government. The national-government scope is small, and the national-government processes are few. Most national scope items and processes are legislative, the next most are executive, and only cases and controversies are judicial.

Most of the scope items in Table 3.1 have to do with preventing or fighting war. Legislative people advise and consent on treaties that could lead to war. Legislative people declare war, fund war, and make all rules for war, which plainly includes rules of engagement. The Commander in Chief commands the people defending against attacks and fighting legislatively-declared wars, following legislatively-determined rules.

Other scope items in Table 3.1 include a very-small number of commerce activities: assure the free flow of goods and services across state lines, govern bankruptcy, coin money and set its value, provide limited exclusive rights for inventors and authors.

Rounding out Table 3.1 are a very-small number of support activities: control naturalization, tax and borrow, judge cases and controversies.

Table 3.1 evokes an earlier time. Even so, the new United States of America were commercially advanced, with the world's highest purchasing

Table 3.1. Constitutional scope

Scope item (Opportunity)	Clause	Type (1=Lead, 2=Offset)			
		States	Nation		
		Legislative	Legislative	Executive	Judicial
Scope not delegated to USA and not prohibited to states	10	1			
Political scope					
Law-of-nations offences	I.8.10		1		
Treaty advice, consent	**II.2.2**		1		
Treaty making	II.2.2			2	
War declaration; marque, reprisal, capture rules	**I.8.11**		1		
Army raising and support up to 2 years	I.8.12		1		
Navy provision and maintenance	I.8.13		1		
Land- and naval-force rules	**I.8.14**		1		
Militia-calling provisions	I.8.15		1		
Militia rules for USA service	I.8.16		1		
Limited government- and military-district laws	I.8.17		1		
Habeas corpus suspension	I.9.2		1		
Treason punishment	III.3.2		1		
Army, Navy, Militia command	II.2.1			2	
Territory laws	IV.3.2		1		
Consent to foreign gifts	I.9.8		1		
Reprieves, pardons except on impeachment	II.2.1			2	

When Powers Are Used

Scope item (Opportunity)	Clause	Type (1=Lead, 2=Offset) States	Nation Legislative	Nation Executive	Nation Judicial
Commercial scope					
Commerce regulations	I.8.3		1		
Bankruptcy laws	I.8.4		1		
Money coinage and valuation	**I.8.5**		**1**		
Weights and measures standards	I.8.5		1		
Counterfeiting punishments	I.8.6		1		
Post offices and post roads	I.8.7		1		
Limited exclusive rights for inventors, authors	**I.8.8**		**1**		
Liquor-transport or -import laws	21.2	1			
Support scope					
Naturalization rules	**I.8.4**		**1**		
Voting laws	**15.2**		**1**		
Voting-tax prohibition laws	24.2		1		
Taxes, duties, imposts, excises	I.8.1		1		
Income-tax laws	16		1		
Borrowing on credit of USA	I.8.2		1		
Slavery, involuntary-servitude laws	13.2		1		
Cases under Constitution, USA laws, treaties	III.2.1				2
Cases on ambassadors, ministers, consuls	III.2.1				2
Cases of admiralty and maritime	III.2.1				2
Controversies involving USA	III.2.1				2
Controversies between states, nations, their people	III.2.1				2

Table 3.2. Constitutional processes

Process (Opportunity)	Clause	Type (1=Lead, 2=Offset) States	Type (1=Lead, 2=Offset) Nation Legislative	Type (1=Lead, 2=Offset) Nation Executive	Type (1=Lead, 2=Offset) Nation Judicial
Legislative processes					
All legislative powers of the USA	I.1		1		
Revenue bill origination	I.7.1		1		
President of Senate	I.3.4			1	
Senate vote when equally divided	I.3.4			1	
Bill signing or objection	I.7.2			2	
Bill reconsideration	I.7.2		2		
Treaty advice, consent	II.2.2		1		
Treatymaking	II.2.2			2	
Amendment proposal	V	1	1		
Amendment ratification	V	1			
Executive processes					
The executive power of the USA	II.1.1			1	
Appointment making	II.2.2			1	
Appointment advice, consent	II.2.2		2		
Inferior-appointments vesting	II.2.2		2		
Senate-recess commissions	II.2.3			1	
Judicial processes					
Judicial power exceptions, regulations	III.2.2		1		
Inferior-court creation	I.8.9		1		
The judicial power of the USA	III.1				1
Impeachment	I.2.5		2		
Impeachment trial	I.3.6		2	2	
Impeachment trial of president	I.3.6		2		2

3.6

When Powers Are Used

power per person—exceeding Great Britain's by 68%.[3.3] The Founders were determined to secure this lead, and they had the world's-best theoretical and practical understanding of political processes.

The legislative processes in Table 3.2 are for lawmaking and amendment. In the legislative processes, executive and state inputs are integral. The vice president presides over the Senate. The president signs or objects to bills (but Congress then reconsiders and passes bills given 2/3 majorities). States can propose amendments, and states ratify amendments.

The executive processes are for appointment of personnel and execution of laws. For appointments, Senate advice and consent are required.

The judicial processes are limited to cases and controversies, and impeachment. Cases and controversies are subject to control by Congress and the states. The states originally delegated the scope, and the states are in control outside the delegated scope except where prohibited by the Constitution. Congress makes exceptions and regulations. Congress creates inferior courts. Subject to these controls, the courts issue opinions. The president then has the only enforcement power.

Impeachment processes have little judicial input. Congress impeaches and tries, and the vice president presides over almost all trials. The chief justice presides over trials of the president. In large part, that's it. That's the supreme law of the land. It's brief, and it's comprehensible. Its boundaries are defined. Its boundaries are not secured, for now.

Securing Boundaries

The Senators and Representatives before mentioned, and the Members of the several State Legislatures, and all executive and judicial Officers, both of the United States and of the several States, shall be bound by Oath or Affirmation, to support this Constitution …[3.4]

The officers … are … bound by their oaths of office to support the Constitution of the United States, and are therefore conscientiously bound to abstain from all acts which are inconsistent with it … If, for instance, the President is required to do any act, he is not only authorized but required to decide for himself, whether, consistently with his constitutional duties, he can do the act.[3.5]

The Constitution binds our government people to secure the Constitution's boundaries on multiple fronts. We can do the same.

When Powers Are Used

We need to do the same. Our government people increasingly succeed in their profession by having certain skills and stamina at speaking, cultivating relationships, and following procedures. And to a remarkable degree, nowadays the procedures they learn on the job involve not following the Constitution but bypassing the Constitution. Unless we call them out for this, this doesn't hurt them, it just hurts us. It's up to us to know what to expect of them, and to make sure that it hurts them if they don't do their jobs for us.

Key opportunities to secure boundaries are shown in the tables in bold.

The executive power, noted in Table 3.2, can do much to secure boundaries immediately.

The executive's environment is target-rich. Administrative bureaus that are said to wield legislative "rulemaking" power are flat unconstitutional. Independent bureaus or congressionally-controlled bureaus that are said to wield independent executive power fall fully under the presidents' power under the Constitution. Judicial opinions outside of specific cases or specific controversies, or outside the enumerated scope of the Constitution, are flat unconstitutional. If you hear anyone in the executive branch say that one of these bureaus or opinions is unconstitutional but then the president still goes ahead and lets it run anyway or still goes ahead and abides by it anyway, know for certain that either the president doesn't even understand what is within his constitutional power to do, or the president is counting on you not noticing.

The executive power of the states has analogous capability to secure boundaries immediately.

The states' environments are broadly target-rich, since the national government's scope is extremely limited. In all matters that fall outside the national government's scope and that have not been prohibited by the Constitution, the states hold all constitutional authority. If you hear anyone in the executive branch of a state say that an activity or opinion is unconstitutional but then the governor still goes ahead and abides by it, know for certain that either the governor doesn't understand what's in his constitutional power to do, or the governor is counting on you not noticing.

The legislative processes can secure boundaries more slowly, but more surely.

Past legislators and executives have created bureaus that have unconstitutionally-delegated legislative and judicial powers, and the current legislators and executive can formally repeal these bureaus.

A vice president, who is elected quite differently than the senators, can substantially redirect the Senate in his constitutional role as the Senate's president (which vice presidents stopped doing as of the rise to power of the Progressive Democrats).[3.6] The Senate has violated the Constitution's requirement for simple-majority voting (without which the vice president's tie-breaking vote could never be cast).[3.7] Either a presiding vice president could restore constitutional simple-majority voting, or senators themselves could vote to restore constitutional simple-majority voting, increasing accountability and bringing faster change for the better.

Either the legislature or the state legislatures can propose amendments, and in either case the state legislatures can ratify them. In much the same way that the most-advisable statutory changes would be repeals, the few advisable amendments would be either repeals or revisions:

- Restore senators to being chosen by the state legislatures.
- Restore the requirement of proportional taxation and no income tax.

- At minimum eliminate the nationwide minimum voting age of 18 (when 90% maturity has only been reached in 15% of brain regions—and only in the regions for primitive functioning, not in the regions for higher reasoning). Ideally, revise the nationwide minimum voting age to at least 25 (when 90% maturity has been reached in 70% of brain regions).[3.8, 3.9]

The judicial processes can secure boundaries in other ways that add useful redundancy and reinforcement.

As Table 3.2 makes plain, the judicial processes are highly controlled by the legislature. The legislature can create exceptions and regulations. These more-narrowly define and secure the boundaries on all national courts, so that the courts can only act legally within this boundary. The legislature creates the inferior national courts and can redesign or eliminate these courts. This more-narrowly defines and secures the boundary on these courts.

Within the applicable boundaries for the various courts, all that the courts can do legally, as empowered by the Constitution, is address

When Powers Are Used

cases and controversies by writing opinions. The courts' opinions have no enforcement power and no legislative power.

And the president, state officers, Congress people, and state legislative people are each bound by oath to support the Constitution, which they can only do by deciding for themselves what is constitutional for them to do and what would be unconstitutional for them to do. These national-level and state-level representatives' every action and every inaction constitutes a further boundary that on an ongoing basis can secure us against the judicial powers.

The judicial powers further include impeachment and impeachment trial, in which the deciding votes to proceed and to conclude are in the hands of the legislative people. Here is yet another means to secure us against unconstitutional actions and inactions of legislators, officers, and judges.

So we have multiple, redundant layers of protection that can secure the boundaries on the government people, to secure the God-given rights of we the people. When seen at a glance in Table 3.1 and Table 3.2, these layers of protection are brief, comprehensible, and muscular.

3.13

Using Offsetting Powers

The offsetting powers that government people can use against other government people are summarized in Table 3.3.

Table 3.3. Offsetting powers in Constitution

Offsetting power (Opportunity)	Clause	States	Nation Legislative	Nation Executive	Nation Judicial
Controlling work in process					
National govt. is supreme on delegated powers	VI.2, 10	✓			
Vice president presides over Senate	I.3.4		✓		
Vice president votes in equally-divided Senate	I.3.4		✓		
President objects to bills	I.7.2		✓		
President blocks treaties	II.2.2		✓		
Congress reconsiders bills	I.7.2			✓	
Senate advises, consents on appointments	II.2.2			✓	
Congress makes judicial exceptions, regulations	III.2.2				✓
Congress creates, redesigns inferior courts	I.8.9				✓
Loss limiting by oath to support Constitution					
State executives disregard if unconstitutional	VI.3		✓	✓	✓
President disregards if unconstitutional	II.1.8		✓		✓
President intervenes if unconstitutional	II.1.8	✓			
State legislators disregard if unconstitutional	VI.3		✓	✓	✓
Congresspeople disregard if unconstitutional	VI.3			✓	✓
Congresspeople intervene if unconstitutional	VI.3	✓			
State judges opine	VI.3		✓	✓	✓
National judges opine	III.1, VI.3	✓	✓	✓	
Loss prevention by impeachment					
House impeaches	I.2.5		✓	✓	✓
Senate tries impeachments	I.3.6, I.3.7		✓	✓	✓
Chief justice presides over impeach. trial of pres.	I.3.6			✓	

Government people have offsetting powers to fix other government people's work in progress.

Government people's oaths to protect or support the Constitution require each person to evaluate constitutionality himself and disregard unconstitutional statutes and opinions, to immediately limit losses.

Congress people have impeachment power over people unworthy of public trust to remove these people now and forever, to prevent future losses.

Work-in-process quality control, loss limiting, and loss prevention—these are comprehensive offsetting powers.

Securing Life, Liberty, and Property

When government people don't perform their roles' scopes, and government people don't secure their role boundaries, the state and national governments have poor boundaries. The government people collectively deny us our rights to life, liberty, and property.

When government people use their powers against other government people, the state and national governments have secure boundaries. The government people independently secure our rights to life, liberty, and property.

3.15

rConstitution Paper 4

Laws That Aren't Readable Aren't Constitutional

CONGRESSMEN IN PRIOR PARTIES have passed, and have left in place, so-called laws that effectively cannot be read, in defiance of the Constitution.

Presidents in prior parties have signed and executed, and have continued to execute, so-called laws that effectively cannot be read, in defiance of the Constitution.[4.1]

A law is a rule plus a sanction (a threatened penalty).[4.2, 4.3]

Nowadays, Congress people's surrogates write bills,[4.4] Congress people pass bills, and presidents sign bills that don't fully define rules and sanctions. Department and agency people follow with regulations that don't fully define rules and sanctions. Later, presidents, department people, and agency people add circulars, memoranda, guidance documents, rulings, and the like, that don't fully define rules and sanctions.[4.5] Ultimately, presidents, department people, and agency people offer chances for consultations that don't fully define rules and sanctions.[4.6] These incomplete rules and sanctions are proliferated by individual government people full-time, and the total population of these people is formidable, so these people threaten every other group and every individual.

A Man's Got to Know His Limitations[4.7]

The threat tends to seem manageable at first.

Our nervous systems give us remarkable abilities to infer patterns and to predict what actions will work for us. In many cases, these abilities operate below the conscious level from the start. This is true of our motor control: we predict where our finger will move and we stimulate our muscles to quickly effect those motions, and we make any fine corrections that might be needed only later as our perceptions of errors arrive after unavoidable built-in delays for vision and touch sensations to make their ways along our nerve conduits.[4.8] In other cases, these abilities quickly

Laws That Aren't Readable

become automatic before we even realize what's happening, and these abilities operate below the conscious level from then on.[4.9] We learn to talk, and walk, and read, and drive. We develop social behaviors that are sophisticated. We learn we can function at levels that are very high.

But when rules and sanctions can be invented at will by millions of government people, or for that matter if they can be invented at will by even one government person, our native abilities fail us. We haven't observed these people in action or this one person in action, so we can't really predict what actions might work for us.

This same unpredictability occurs when rules and sanctions form a corpus so large that we can't sample them fully enough. Here too, we don't have enough observations to guide us, so we can't really predict what actions might work for us. Here too, our native abilities fail us.

Before that, the government people's native abilities fail them. They compensate right away—the same way we compensate later—by upping their numbers. Judges' native abilities are augmented by hand-picked staff lawyers, by outside lawyers who prepare summary briefs, and by outside lawyers who answer questions in real time in court. Presidents' native abilities are augmented

4.3

by hand-picked staff, confirmed staff, and other at least nominally-responsive staff—a total population that's formidable. Congress people's native abilities are augmented by hand-picked staff, by their houses' offices of legislative counsel, and by lobbyists.[4.4] State-government people's native abilities are augmented in all the same ways.

When a statute is ill-defined or oppressively thick, or when an administrative department or agency is long-lived, it becomes certain that the resulting outpouring cascade of partially-defined rules and sanctions is produced without any single person having read and comprehended the whole cascade's corpus. And it is certain that no single person has read and comprehended the national government's whole corpus of rules and sanctions.

Maybe reading and comprehending all of those rules and sanctions sounds unimaginable. This is a problem, and it's dangerous.

People have delegated to their elected representatives the responsibility to represent the people's interests. And these interests cannot possibly be represented by elected representatives who vote or sign to feed and grow rules and sanctions that they can't possibly read and comprehend. The fact that elected representatives can't possibly read and comprehend the corpus means that the

Laws That Aren't Readable

corpus can't possibly result from constitutional, republican stewardship.

Note that the staff people and outside people who augment the representatives' native abilities are not elected representatives. Being people, they are self-interested. They can reasonably be anticipated to be highly interested in keeping their jobs, and in doing more of the same kinds of tasks they're sure they're good at doing. These self-interests very likely incline these people to have a high interest in keeping their jobs and to have a high interest in propagating more of the same rules and sanctions, regardless of what rules and sanctions people actually need or want from their elected representatives.

How large a corpus of national rules and sanctions could possibly result from constitutional, republican stewardship? In the House of Representatives, the terms in office are only 2 years. Say that these representatives start out in office by reading the national corpus of rules and sanctions full time for a month. Rules and sanctions would be hard to fully understand by simply reading straight through, and would be impossible to remember very well. Even so, this full, straight-through reading would provide a modest overview understanding of the whole corpus of rules and sanctions. How big a corpus would they be physiologically able to read straight through in a month? The physiological upper bound—when readers fixate on most of the words in a text and occasionally look back at previously-read words—is net forward movement of around 300 words per minute.[4.10] That means that responsible republican representatives who read the national rules and sanctions full-time for a month could finish a complete corpus that numbers around 3 million words:

$$1\ month \cdot 300\ \frac{words}{min} \cdot 60\ \frac{min}{hr} \cdot 40\ \frac{hr}{week} \cdot \frac{52\ weeks}{12\ months}$$
$$= 3{,}120{,}000\ words$$

Nothing Exceeds like Excess[4.11]

In reality, the national rules and sanctions in the United States Code number 22 million words,[4.12] the national rules and sanctions in the Code of Federal Regulations number 103 million words,[4.13] and the national rules and sanctions in national case law—based on the ratios for tax laws[4.14]—number around 633 million words. Case-by-case guidance that's nonbinding on the government people likely adds further national rules and sanctions that run few additional words but that require preparation, meeting, actions, and continued meeting for ongoing risk mitigation.

Laws That Aren't Readable

Leaving aside this latter case-by-case guidance, the total national rules and sanctions might number around 758 million words. Reading this corpus full-time with no holidays would take 20 years.

Given coffee and plenty of oxytocin to help this repetitive work be more tolerable,[4.15] a hypothetical reader would gain a passing familiarity with where to start to re-read when beginning to address a given problem. Even so, much would have changed during those 20 years. The reader would return to the older material with no more knowledge of its present state than the legendary Rip Van Winkle had about the present state of the world when he reawakened after sleeping for 20 years.[4.16]

The Congress people and presidents who go through the motions of representing their constituents in the face of these schemes aren't fooling anyone. Voters don't believe that the 22 million words of bills predefined the 103 million words of regulations, or that the 103 million words of regulations predefined the 633 million words of case law. Any government that generates law that the government people themselves need augmenting staff to cope with in narrow tranches, and that the nation's people can't adequately sample and predict, so that the nation's people need to engage well-studied specialists to cope with it in narrow tranches, is not representative and is not constitutional, but rather is plainly tyrannical.

Multiple Layers of Protection[4.17]

Tyranny calls for a full-court press.

Judges have a generally-sorry record in the United States of America, but there were once times of tyranny in England during which judges weighed in and strengthened the legislatures against the administrative powers exerted by the kings.[4.18] Each judge has a chance to add to this fine legacy.

Presidents have asymmetric powers under the Constitution. They are constitutionally constrained to only execute laws, and to not exercise legislative powers.[4.19] Meanwhile, they are constitutionally bound to not execute unconstitutional laws.[4.20] And the executive power is vested not in the creations of congresses or in the creations of judges, but in presidents alone.[4.21] Any president, at any time, even using only very-rough judgment of how unconstitutional the current administrative departments and agencies are, has substantial, immediate power to not continue these current tyrannies even slightly.

Congress people have the most power under the Constitution in scope areas that the states delegated to the national government. All legislative powers granted via the Constitution are vested in Congress people.[4.19] Unlike presidents, Congress people can change legal statutes—the only multi-case law that is constitutional—and have their changes be preserved for some time by Senate people who remain in office, and be preserved for even more time through the constitutional government's various offsetting powers that people in various roles can use independently of the other branches to forestall the reintroduction of tyrannies.

State-government people have the most power under the Constitution in general, and all power in scope areas reserved through the Constitution and delegated through state constitutions to the states. For the most part, this power goes unused. People don't recognize that the states have this power, and state-government people aspire to national government office and don't want to upset the people who are already there. This is an outstanding opportunity for change. Any state-government people who choose to can simply follow their understanding of the Constitution, as they are bound to do by their oath to uphold the Constitution.[4.20] Any state-government people who choose to can resist as many of the unconstitutional actions of the national government as they choose to. Congress and the national courts, even the Supreme Court, have no enforcement powers. The only enforcement power that can be wielded against state-government people is under the control of presidents, and presidents are constrained by budgets and by political considerations. The national-government people's limitations were demonstrated by Prohibition.

Each of these groups of people needs a game plan. Here, the same strategy applies for all. The thing to focus on first and on an ongoing basis is the money.

Stop Fueling the Fire

The overall corpus of rules and sanctions has a fundamental impact to the extent that it can't all be read. Its impact is more direct when it is read and it includes rules.

A proxy for the rules and sanctions in the overall corpus is offered by the regulations' overall count of restrictions. Restrictions are where free and voluntary cooperation is overridden by force of law using words like "shall" or "must".

The regulations' overall count of restrictions has been increasing for years, as shown in Figure 4.1 below.

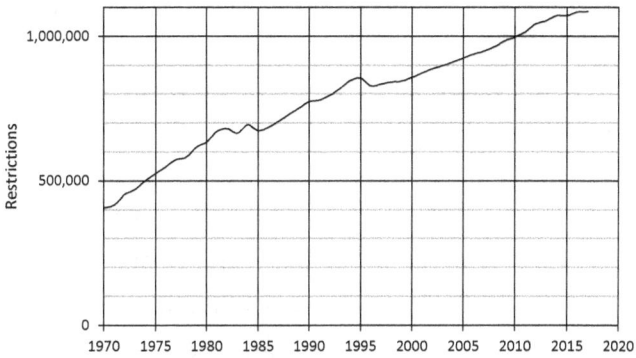

Figure 4.1. Agency restrictions have built up considerably and have kept trending up.[4.22]

These are unconstitutional controls, so legally their count should be zero. Overall, in 47 years their count increased by a factor of 2.7. Across every decade, the trend was up.

This is to be expected. If the number of agency people was zero, restrictions would remain constant. Since the number of agency people is greater than zero, restrictions can be expected to increase. During lulls, restrictions can be expected to keep being developed and be issued later.

The obvious antidote is to stop doing more harm. Eliminate these rulers and their enablers.

Judges' native abilities are augmented by staff lawyers. Eliminate these lawyers. Judges' native abilities are augmented by outside lawyers who prepare summary briefs and by outside lawyers who answer questions in real time in court. Eliminate these practices.

Presidents' native abilities are augmented by hand-picked staff, confirmed staff, and other at least nominally-responsive staff. Eliminate the national criminal laws that don't involve the few enumerated national powers like controlling the army and the navy. Eliminate the staff lawyers. Eliminate whole unconstitutional departments and agencies. To people who claim that commerce needs to be regulated, point out that empirically in the United States of America, under the guise of preventing states from interfering with commerce, the national government has interfered with mutually-beneficial interchanges of goods and services on mutually-agreed terms on a scale that no states have ever approached; that likely no states will ever even threaten to restrain trade on a scale so significant; and that if states ever do begin to restrain trade materially, Congress will still have constitutional authority to react proportionally after the fact. Point out that continuing to act preemptively with disproportional

Laws That Aren't Readable

force plainly violates the level of commerce power that's consonant with the other limited powers that were delegated to the national government by the states when they ratified the Constitution.

Congress people's native abilities are augmented by their staff and by their houses' offices of legislative counsel. Eliminate these positions.

State-government people retain great power under the Constitution. Any people who choose can assert as much of that power as they choose. The more widespread the constitutional assertions of power, the less force the national government will be able to counter with.

Any notion that we can't return to constitutional republican government is not just tyranny, but also simply unsupportable.

We already have a fine body of national law: the Constitution. All by itself, the Constitution nicely sets out the role that's desirable for the national government, puts in place people to opine on cases and controversies, and puts in place offsetting powers for the people's representatives to address unwise opinions and any more-general policies that are in-scope for the national government.

Nothing sharpens the mind like failing at what you've been doing, and having to return to fundamentals and rebuild from there. Even politicians can change and return to only adding value, if we stop letting them destroy value.

Our forefathers did this once before. Now it's up to us.

rConstitution Paper 5

Laws That Direct the Executive or Direct the Judiciary Are Unconstitutional

CONGRESSMEN IN PRIOR PARTIES have passed, and have left in place, so-called laws that direct the executive branch or the judicial branch, in defiance of the Constitution.

Presidents in prior parties have signed and executed, and have continued to execute, so-called laws that direct the executive branch or the judicial branch, in defiance of the Constitution.[5.1]

It's tough to make laws that are good.

One approach that makes writing and thinking clearer and ultimately better is to eliminate needless words.[5.2, 5.3, 5.4]

What words are needless in law is not immediately obvious. Law creation is the power that's first and foremost, law execution is later and lesser, and opining on cases is last and least. Given the law creators' first-mover advantage, the legislative people who pass laws and the presidents who sign laws have an opportunity to try to pack into laws pretty much whatever they want to. But opportunity is not license.

What's needed in a law—what defines a law as a law—are small, specific bits of information: a rule coupled with a sanction (a threatened penalty).[5.5, 5.6] If a law is of the kind that's most desirable, it also doesn't show favoritism but rather treats every individual alike, and this makes it even simpler.[5.7]

Don't Grab Executive Power

One element that's good to exclude from a law is any rule that directs the executive branch. This is unconstitutional. The executive power is vested in presidents alone.[5.8]

Governments are organizations that, apart from some exceptional times long ago in our nation's history, have never been high-functioning,

Laws That Direct

so it's understandable that their proper functioning is not well-studied. But executive power is well-studied and well-articulated in business. Business executive power manages three major functional areas: finance, marketing, and operations.[5.9] The government is a monopoly, so the Constitution doesn't address marketing. The remaining government executive power addressed by the Constitution is in the areas of finance and operations management.

In finance of the national government, the Constitution empowers Congress people to vote on and presidents to sign bills that provide supervisory control of revenues and appropriations.[5.10, 5.11] Finance people in business exercise such supervisory control by setting high-level budget targets by business division.

Historically, the national-government people also set strictly high-level targets, at first. The first general appropriation act in 1789, which was voted on and signed by representatives who understood the new Constitution well, listed single lump-sum line-item appropriations for civil-list expenses, war-department expenses, discharge of treasury warrants, and pensions to invalids. These four line items constituted the whole budget.[5.12]

Finance people in business generally respect operations people's boundaries, and do not cross over and infringe on operations management. When there are exceptions in business, the business adds less value and its customers vote with their feet to go elsewhere. Congress people, though, no longer respect the boundary between appropriation power and executive power, and presidents no longer act to secure this boundary.

Congress people claim executive control of operations by dividing and conquering. They divide into appropriation subcommittees, and using their seats of power in these fiefdoms they barter with other Congress people. Every Congress person stands to gain a tailored set of appropriations from various subcommittees that will best polish up his résumé for his next reelection.

No one Congress person has individual bottom-line responsibility for all appropriations; and when everyone's in charge, no one's in charge. Such problems with divided responsibility—for example, inability to pin down which specific individuals are accountable for an executive group's actions—led the Constitutional Convention people and the state ratifying-convention people to not vote to adopt George Mason's proposed three-person executive group, but to instead vote to have a single president.[5.13] Our founding design people showed by their discussions and their actions that they would vigorously reject what's the customary practice today. Today, the president's executive power of operations management is largely grabbed away and diffused across the whole lot of the Congress people.

Once every Congress person has lined up all the bartered goods he can grab, they all come together in their two houses and vote for the appropriations bills. The president, offered a golden opportunity to avoid constitutionally-mandated individual accountability, then signs the appropriations bills.

The Congress people's power grab extends well into the basic executive power of operations management. So-called laws unconstitutionally grab control over organizing the national government's operations into departments and agencies, organizing these divisions into further subdivisions, terms of employment, and assigning certain tasks. So-called laws unconstitutionally grab control over setting implementation schedules.

If appropriations would be restored to being a high-level supervisory control by Congress people voting and presidents signing as required by the

Constitution, and if the remaining executive power would be restored to presidents as required by the Constitution, much would change. A Congress person's key tasks would be exercising a small amount of high-level supervisory control through appropriations, and beyond that simply improving laws to support the Constitution. A president's key task would be operations management. His key performance metrics would be the risk-weighted likely total loss from war preparation and war, the effectiveness of enforcement of laws, and the efficiency of operations.

Such accountability for operations is already designed into the president's job by the Constitution. The simple step needed to restore this accountability is to eliminate from laws all the unconstitutional rules that direct the executive branch.

Don't Grab Judicial Power

A second element that's good to exclude from a law is any rule that directs the judicial branch. This is unconstitutional in all but rare instances. As a rule, the judicial power is vested in the courts alone.[5.14]

Congress people can ordain and establish inferior courts, can make exceptions to appellate

Laws That Direct

jurisdictions, and can make regulations on appellate matters.[5.14, 5.15]

Each of these powers is valuable but rare. Congress people ordained and established inferior courts long ago, and they modify these courts rarely. Congress people could greatly rein in court overreaches by making exceptions to appellate jurisdictions, but even if they would do this they would still be making exceptions rarely. Congress people could greatly strengthen property rights by making regulations on appellate jurisdictions, but even if they would do this they would still be making these regulations rarely.

One big reason that Congress people make these regulations rarely may be simply that the judicial regulation that was planned for in Article III looks like it instead got worked out immediately afterwards in the Bill of Rights. In Article III and in the Bill of Rights, the Constitution itself regulates the judicial branch on maximum jurisdiction, juries, venues, treason, search warrants, grand juries, double jeopardy, self-incrimination, due process, just compensation, speedy trial, charges, witnesses, defense counsel, appeal facts, bail, fines, and punishments.[5.16]

To sum up about the constitutional powers of Congress people over the judicial branch that were outlined and discussed above: much is settled, and new uses are rare.

But meanwhile Congress people have grabbed judicial power unconstitutionally on a massive scale. Throughout departments and agencies, Congress people created administrative adjudicatory bodies that exercise judicial power without complying with the Constitution's regulations.

These unconstitutional judicial bodies can actively seek out cases, hear nonstandard evidence, use nonstandard processes, consider "social justice," require initial appeal inside the agency, and exert spreading, corrupting influence on outside appeals courts.[5.17]

On these unconstitutional grabs of judicial power, things are all wrong, and new abuses are common.

Simple Rules for a Complex World[5.18]

Simple rules provide clean go/no-go tests. They provide a bright line with no gray area, which handles most cases cleanly.

The unconstitutional grabs of power discussed above can be prevented using a simple rule that provides two clean go/no-go tests: A bill shall contain no rule that directs the executive branch or that directs the judicial branch.

Laws That Direct

If a bill contains any rule that directs the executive branch, then the bill fails the first test cleanly, and further investigation is unnecessary.

If a bill contains any rule that directs the judicial branch, then the bill fails the second test cleanly, and further investigation is simple. In the rare exception when a bill fails the second test but is still constitutional because the bill is an exercise of an Article III power, Congress people are well aware that they're exercising an Article III power. This rare exception is handled essentially automatically.

Bills that direct the executive branch or that direct the judicial branch can be avoided very simply. Eliminating needless words that would direct the executive branch or the judicial branch will prevent much unconstitutional power-grabbing very simply.

The remaining rules and sanctions may need to be worked out through factfinding work, compromises, and even trial and error; simple tests don't mean that rule and sanction choices are easy.

But defining a problem well helps you solve a problem well.

rConstitution Paper 6

Laws That Delegate Legislative Authority Are Unconstitutional

CONGRESSMEN IN PRIOR PARTIES have passed, and have left in place, so-called laws that delegate legislative authority to issue so-called regulations that plainly have the force of laws, in defiance of the Constitution.

Presidents in prior parties have signed and executed, and have continued to execute, so-called laws that delegate legislative authority to issue so-called regulations that plainly have the force of laws, in defiance of the Constitution.[6.1]

All legislative powers granted in the Constitution are vested in a House of Representatives and in a Senate.[6.2] The House of Representatives represents the individual people equally, and the Senate represents the states equally.[6.3, 6.4, 6.5] These Congress representatives likely differ from the individual people and the state people in talent, virtue, and wealth, but the representatives were expected to be kept responsive to the individual people and to the states through elections.[6.6]

Elections don't automatically have this consequence. All representatives now come from oligopoly political parties, and most of these representatives' actions aren't responsive.[6.7]

Voters need to know what it looks like when representatives' actions are responsive. One action that's responsive—and that was a key advance of the Constitution—is that representative legislators write every law.

The Fountainhead Is Laws

A law is a rule plus a sanction (a threatened penalty).[6.8, 6.9] Anything more isn't law, and anything less isn't law. This is true even when a non-law is labeled as a law, and even when a law is labeled as not a law.

Instead of writing every law, current representatives delegate to others the task of writing laws.

Laws, after all, have consequences. If a rule plus a threatened penalty has to be written to

Laws That Delegate

change people's actions, then that change comes at a cost to those people.

For representatives, delegating is an actual free lunch. The representative takes credit for fixing a visible problem by coming up with the solution. The representative evades blame for forcing people to bear new costs. And the representative ingratiates himself to campaign donors and voters by going to bat for them case-by-case against the other people who are trying to force the donors and voters to pay a new cost.

Representatives delegate the task of writing laws by creating unconstitutional grants of power.

This actual delegating is dressed up to look constitutional. Legislators go through the motions of passing bills, and presidents go through the motions of signing the bills into so-called laws.

The resulting unconstitutional grants of power are then unconstitutionally implemented by others in government.

Sooner or later, the implementers come to understand first-hand that grants are not laws.

The 1970 Clean Air Act, wrote former National Resources Defense Council attorney David Schoenbrod, "regulates government rather than sources of pollution."[6.10] This description is deceptively benign, given that such acts regulate government not by restraining government, but by expanding government.

Even though it's deceptive, though, Prof. Schoenbrod's wording that the Act "regulates government" does describe the most-overt characteristic of the grants. The grants typically consist of overwhelming masses of words, words that unconstitutionally direct presidents and unconstitutionally bypass judges.

But the grants summon up their strongest power just by specifying a name and a charter.

Blank Checks to Coerce

Much like grants of land, these grants of government scope reach out into the unsecured space of all human activity to grab and stake out new claim locations in which to grow the national government. A grant's name and charter mislead the state-government people into unconstitutional submission. Presidents and judges line up to unconstitutionally collude, and bask in media fawning. Every other organized group—even the largest corporation—is too unprotected and small to be able to resist and prosper. The national-government people's strongest power grab comes from just showing up and working the room.

Laws That Delegate

Legislators who delegate legislative power are like many executives when the new personal computers first became available in the executive suites. Many executives took it as a mark of status that executives don't type; typing is the work of secretaries. Legislators turn their work over to agency people.

Agency people can and do develop unconstitutional laws called regulations.

But also, agency people innovate in their own sphere of action, the same way that engineers innovate in their own sphere of action most quickly and most effectively, by reusing proven components:[6.11] agency people, like legislators, innovate by themselves delegating. This way agency people, like legislators, empower themselves to take credit for creating solutions, evade blame for new costs, and work for donations. Donations valued by agency people include research funding and future jobs in government-friendly organizations.

Innovation by people in business necessarily increases efficiency and increases quality, because people in business need the resulting products to be freely chosen by customers. Innovation by people in government could similarly increase efficiency and increase quality. After all, people in government stand to benefit if their products are freely chosen by voters. In practice, though, voters' choices are severely limited by current parties. As a result, voters have very-little control over representatives in government and no control over people in government agencies. The direct result of voters' lack of control is that agency people innovate not to add value but rather to grab more power.

This power grab by agency people—producing new types of unconstitutional laws and further delegations, frustrating enforcement of the Constitution and frustrating industry countermoves—involves considerable innovation. Each time one form of unconstitutional lawmaking is threatened or seems too limiting, the agency people come up with a new innovation.

The founding form of unconstitutional lawmaking was formal rulemaking using hearings. Next came formal adjudication, building up precedents to form unconstitutional case law. In the late 1960s, informal rulemaking, also called notice-and-comment rulemaking, skipped hearings and went straight to publishing full-blown plans in the *Federal Register*. Later came hybrid rulemaking, where informal rulemaking was combined with other procedures, usually added by Congress. Very-informal rulemaking skipped notice and comment by claiming that the agency

Laws That Delegate

people are acting with good cause. Negotiated rulemaking brought in favored business people or interest-group people during drafting of unconstitutional law. Standards adoption took work done for internal coordination by trade associations, professional associations, producer cooperatives, or international bodies and transmogrified that work into unconstitutional law. In the 1980s, interpretation bypassed the need to claim to be acting with good cause. Later came guidance, best practices, policies, advice, briefs, demands, arm-twisting threats, determinations, penalties, taxes, tariffs, administrative fees, nuisance declarations, licensing, and waivers.[6.12] And further variant tools-of-the-art keep coming.[6.13]

One tool that's chilling is radio silence. Consumer Financial Protection Bureau Director Richard Cordray said the bureau wouldn't issue any regulations that define exactly what actions or practices violate the bureau's unconstitutional law.[6.14, 6.15]

Many variants of these unconstitutional laws get accreted into bundles—or get withheld—agency by agency, by each agency's people.

Agency people are attracted to an agency's stated purpose; they're selected to fit the agency's activities; and if the attraction was valid and the

6.7

selection was valid, they stay.[6.16] Their job isn't to add economic value that people choose to pay for, it's to add political value that people choose to vote for. They're in sales.[6.17] They work inside a thicket of unconstitutional laws; they watch political appointees and their priorities come and go; and they serve themselves, activists, Congress people, congressional staff, presidents, presidential staff, and media people.[6.18]

Their customer service to we the people, compared to the customer service in nine other industry sectors, ranks dead last—below cable TV, electric utilities, and airlines.[6.19] This only makes sense: they don't work for us.

They work primarily for themselves and for Congress people. In either case this has the same serious consequence.

Back Scratch Fever[6.20]

Congress people are each little fiefdoms that barter with other Congress fiefdoms to assemble individual sales displays for their next reelections. Agency people are each little fiefdoms that barter with the little Congress fiefdoms, selling inside-sales support in exchange for budgets.

Even the most-powerful Congress person is only required to sell his services to voters in his

Laws That Delegate

state or district and later to his fellow rulers, and is never required to sell his services to voters across the nation. Even the most-powerful agency person is only required to provide inside-sales support to Congress people and presidents who are the outside-sales people, and is never required to directly sell his services to voters anywhere.

Each Congress person and each agency person is only required to look after his own fiefdom interests. None of these rulers are required to look after the total. That's what's required of presidents. Presidents alone have the executive power.[6.21]

Presidents, though, don't use this constitutional executive power. Like Congress people who take credit but shift blame by delegating lawmaking power to agency people, presidents take credit but shift blame by leaving this executive power to agency people.

Note that this leaves presidents without much to do, kind of like vice presidents, who the Founders worried didn't have any job to do. Presidents mostly just sign or veto bills that unconstitutionally grant more government scope, conduct wars unconstitutionally, and sell: sell themselves, sell big government.

Congress people clearly take the first-mover advantage when they pass so-called laws that delegate lawmaking. Presidents clearly collude when they sign the so-called laws. Unconstitutional agencies get raised up, and they stay standing unless presidents, governors, other Congress people, state legislators, or judges make countermoves using the powers delegated to them from the start by the people.

Constitutional Remedies

Thankfully, the people in each of these roles swear oaths to support the Constitution.[6.22, 6.23] Each of these people has constitutional powers to counter these unconstitutional power grabs by past and current Congress people and presidents. Any president and any governor can and, by oath, should immediately stop executing any and all unconstitutional statutes and agency laws. Any Congress people can quickly vote to formally repeal these already-unconstitutional statutes and laws. Any judges can quickly opine that these statutes and laws are unconstitutional.[6.24]

We the people have a supreme law that governs here, and this Constitution is clear from the start: all legislative powers granted in the Constitution are vested in a House of Representatives and in a Senate.[6.2]

rConstitution Paper 7

Laws That Mislead Are Unconstitutional

CONGRESSMEN IN PRIOR PARTIES *have passed, and have left in place, so-called laws that are misleading, providing support for others to legislate by interpretation, in defiance of the Constitution. Presidents in prior parties have signed and executed, and have continued to execute, so-called laws that are misleading, providing support for others to legislate by interpretation, in defiance of the Constitution.*[7.1]

If Government Was Small

How might people develop and utilize pharmaceutical drugs if government people just secured people's rights to life and property?[7.2, 7.3]

7.1

People's rights might be secured best if government people enforce just two requirements. First, drug patent monopolies could be provided but with a requirement that patent owners openly share, in real time, all in-house documentation of manufacturing-process details and clinically-relevant data. Second, if a consumer used a drug properly and the drug caused harm, the manufacturer could be held strictly liable.[7.4] Given these simple value-adding ground rules, all other value would be added naturally by business people and customers.

People in drug companies would focus more on novel drug targets.[7.5] They would discover more new drug molecules.[7.6, 7.7] They would share their safety lab test, animal study, and healthy-volunteer study methods. The methods that were the most sensitive and most efficient would soon get used universally. Products that passed through this initial screening would quickly get released.

In-use safety monitoring and efficacy monitoring would be accomplished as decentralized open collaborations among drug-company people, big-data experts, epidemiologists, product reviewers, healthcare specialists, and customers. Drug-company people would be free to optimize sales volumes of initial product releases to balance revenue rewards against risks of financial overexposure from latent side effects. Customers and healthcare specialists would decide for themselves whether potential leading-edge efficacy was a reward that, for them, outweighed a new drug's somewhat-greater efficacy uncertainty and safety risk.[7,8] These decisions would be informed not only the way they're informed now, with help from drug-company marketing people and drug-company physicians, but also with further help from big-data experts, epidemiologists, and product reviewers. Early on, the healthcare specialists who would be the most comfortable with working with elevated risk and uncertainty would normally include the most-superexpert and most-expert diagnosticians: the specialist doctors who interact with patients most effectively, recognize side effects most quickly, and take action most effectively.

Safety side effects that are relatively rare would still elude prerelease testing and would still turn up at small rates only as use spread widely to much-larger populations. These side effects would be mitigated much more effectively through the open communication, very-high level of collaboration, and engagement of data specialists awash in data and funded by interested drug manufacturers, healthcare specialists, and customers.

Efficacy would normally be discerned not by comparing to the effects of inactive placebos but rather by comparing to the effects of the leading alternative drugs. Efficacy would normally be discerned not by selecting patients who are likely to show the most improvement but rather by observing patients who have all-available severities and co-occurring conditions. Efficacy would normally be discerned not from company-funded small samples of patients but from self-funded large, complete populations of patients. And efficacy would normally be discovered not only for a single target condition but also for any co-occurring conditions that were present in patients coincidentally.

Economy would improve steadily as drug-company people made large and small process changes freely, to manufacture more efficiently and to improve quality.

Healthcare treatment would improve steadily as therapeutic drug options were developed that had more-varied action, worked better, and were even safer. Healthcare diagnosis would steadily improve as the greater therapeutic options led to better isolation and treatment of individual conditions, and in turn to earlier recognition of co-occurring conditions, by specialists at all

Laws That Mislead

skill levels—from expert teachers at university medical centers, to practitioners at standardized retail outlets.

Such outcomes can be reasonably anticipated because evidence is available on how people collaborate to add value in sectors that are freer—for example, the sector providing computers, and the sector providing fast foods. Also, evidence is available from natural experiments in the ways drugs are worked on at various places in the world, and in the ways drugs have been worked on at past times in history. Large decentralized systems—such as people working with the Internet, and people collaborating on large open-software projects like the programming language Python—have proven amazingly capable of uncovering threats quickly and responding effectively. Such systems offer threat detection that's as local and individuated as possible, combined with threat response that's as versatile and effective as possible. When safety depends on rapid detection and response—with fault tolerance and resilience—a system ideally will include the largest-feasible array of premium components such as the Mayo Clinic's skilled symptom recognition and diagnosis, and the Johnson & Johnson people's rapid response to the 1982 Tylenol murders. With large, open systems, whenever relevant new data emerge anywhere in the system, such systems diffuse data across the system widely and rapidly, and the system improves rapidly.

When Laws Mislead

The FDA people don't sell themselves as small, helpful property-rights securers in a complex value-adding system. Instead, the way they frame it, "FDA is responsible for protecting the public health by assuring the safety, efficacy and security of human and veterinary drugs..."[7.9]

Never mind security; safety and efficacy are not produced, assured, or the responsibility of FDA people.

Safety is an emergent characteristic of the entire interconnected-network system of drug developers and customers. Safety can't be known anywhere in the system until the relevant knowledge emerges somewhere in the system. At times, there are unknown unknowns.[7.10]

Safety tests miss some effects on humans. Side effects include some effects too rare to be seen until a drug is utilized by a large population.

Even after rare effects first emerge in individual cases, the connection to the drug has to be suspected and recognized, and this safety knowledge

Laws That Mislead

has to be communicated openly throughout the system. Until then, any parts of the system that the knowledge hasn't reached remain unsafe. Any people this safety knowledge hasn't reached are less likely to connect the use of a drug to additional cases of a rare side effect. Also, any people this safety knowledge hasn't reached are unable to help recognize whether the people who develop a rare side effect have in common some necessary precondition, so that screening for this precondition would allow everyone to avoid the drug's rare side effect and would allow many people to still obtain the drug's benefit.

System components can interact in ways that make safety increase, or in ways that make safety decrease. For instance, the manufacturer's people's prescribing information about mechanism of action and a healthcare specialist's knowledge of a patient's individual vulnerabilities can work together to increase safety. But the prescribing information and the specialist's limited knowledge under time pressure can instead combine to lead to actions that reduce safety.

In the same way, efficacy is also an emergent characteristic of the system of people interacting.

The FDA people and other government people make themselves part of the system, and this changes the system's characteristics. The results depend on how the FDA people and other government people interact with the other people in the system.

As set out in the FDA people's mission statement, the FDA people don't secure property rights, and they don't collaborate. What things do the FDA people do? When the drug development and utilization system first generated new information about sanitation in drug manufacturing, toxicity of diethylene glycol, and toxicity of thalidomide, people other than the FDA people responded by changing development processes, starting to change notification and recall processes, and starting to search for elusive animal tests to forewarn about thalidomide's toxicity to humans in the womb.[7.11] In each case, the new information led to system safety improvements from that point onward, independently of the FDA people.

The FDA people did help retrieve the diethylene glycol product.[7.12] Also, the FDA people, although unaware of thalidomide's toxicity to humans in the womb, still slowed down thalidomide's use on USA patients.[7.13]

But mainly the FDA people responded by working with Congress people and presidents to invent larger grants of government scope. The sanitation information was turned into a grant to prevent poisoning, which didn't prevent the diethylene glycol poisoning. The diethylene glycol information was turned into a grant to prereview safety data, which didn't prevent the thalidomide side effects. The thalidomide information was turned into a grant to preapprove efficacy,[7.11] which in the hands of the FDA people greatly slowed improvement in safety and efficacy.

Property rights were and are significantly destroyed. From 1968 to 1972 and beyond, the FDA people overrode drug-company people's prior practice and doctors' clinical judgments, and, using methods that were secretive, misleading, and arbitrary, the FDA people removed drugs from the market on a scale that was massive. Of all drugs in use in 1968, the FDA people destroyed the patent rights and the generics value of about 1/2.[7.14] The FDA people delay doctors' normal prescribing of new drugs until manufacturers complete one specific type of efficacy test, plus FDA reviews.[7.15] This destroys the potential value of having these drugs in use earlier—and drugs could be in use earlier, on average, by as much as 8 years.[7.16, 7.17] Further, allowing drugs to be in use earlier would make competitive drugs get developed faster.

In the FDA-warped environment, people in drug companies have been focusing disproportionately more on a single family of known drug targets that has yielded only 20% of the top 50 drugs worldwide.[7.5] They've been discovering fundamental new therapeutic action in only a small proportion of new drugs, around 4%.[7.18] Since they added the FDA people's required one specific type of efficacy test, their innovative-capacity utilization (based on new chemical entities produced per decade) has been just 37%.[7.19] They work with the FDA people to keep their test methods and data controlled tightly and released very selectively. Their ratio of marketing to basic research is now 19 to 1.[7.6] And yet they're not allowed to market new uses that doctors regularly discover, which leaves lots of value destroyed.[7.15]

In-use safety monitoring is done largely in secrecy by doctors facing time pressure, drug-company people facing liability pressure, and FDA people facing publicity pressure. In-use efficacy monitoring is done largely coincidentally by doctors facing time pressure. Drug-company people, faced with huge sunk costs, and needing to recoup most of those costs within considerably-shortened effective patent lives, are safest innovating relatively little, marketing heavily, and adding

Laws That Mislead

patents over time so that patent lives effectively get longer. Customers face extreme rationing of new therapeutic options, and even then are at risk of receiving inactive placebos. Customers almost all have to wait much longer before they're legally allowed by the FDA people to buy the drugs that are the best available. Customers far too often don't even have that much time left.[7.20]

Safety side effects still occur. The people directly involved are a working group that's relatively small, they work largely in secret, and their self-interests can conflict. In this setup, information is not necessarily recognized rapidly and communicated rapidly.

Efficacy is discerned by comparing to inactive placebos, at very-high costs, with very-long delays. Compared to customer-funded tests against the leading alternative drugs in the normal patient population, the FDA-required company-funded efficacy tests against placebos in relatively-few patients are underpowered, so they're more likely to miss significant effects, and they cost much more. Compared to how efficacies would be understood in an environment of doctors and customers working together freely and doctors collaborating freely, efficacies other than for the therapeutic use that was initially envisioned are investigated rarely, uncovered rarely, and communicated poorly.

Economy in manufacturing worsens steadily, as drug-company people are strongly incentivized by FDA people to keep processes frozen in their original form forever.

Property Is Destroyed

Safety, efficacy, and economy are just features of the overall value of drugs as property. When property is destroyed and it belongs to companies, companies can only recover and stay in business by increasing the prices of other products, which must be paid by customers. When property is secure for customers, customers gain even more added value, since customers only trade money for products if, to them, their money is worth less and the products are worth more. For customers, drugs are perhaps the most-valuable category of property on the planet: of all welfare gains achieved by people worldwide during the 20th century, new pharmaceutical drugs accounted for as much as 1/2.[7.21] Such added value provides excellent cover for people in government to grab new scope and engage in activities that are destructive.[7.22] If property rights to drugs would be kept secure from the FDA people, the potential gain for

Laws That Mislead

all people would be more miracles than we can imagine. Great payoffs can come from vigilance against government scope creep.

The government scope creep described above is built on a foundation that's instructively weak. The statute requires only "substantial evidence that the drug will have the effect it purports or is represented to have." This illusory standard "actually promises nothing because it leaves to the [drug sponsor] the choice of performance or nonperformance."[7.23] Upon this statute, FDA people erected their preferred so-called gold standard of blind, randomized trials against placebos, destroying a large fraction of the pharmaceutical industry's capacity for innovation starting in 1962, and compounding to become an ever-larger fraction destroyed over time.

Congress people investigate approved drugs on which safety problems emerge, so FDA people can and do enhance their reputations by reducing approvals.[7.24] And as the discussion above has shown, reducing approvals hurts us all. It brings higher development costs, fewer breakthroughs, fewer drugs, and longer delays until treatments are made available. Property rights are destroyed. Gains in public health are destroyed. People needlessly suffer and die. If we were free from

FDA people's interference, people would live better and longer.[7.7]

This example shows why Congress people and presidents shouldn't pass and leave in place laws that mislead and can be used to mislead.

A law is strictly a rule plus a sanction (a threatened penalty).[7.25, 7.26] A so-called law that contains non-law statements of any kind defies the Constitution by incentivizing people other than Congress people to write unconstitutional laws.

Budgets give these people the means. Non-law statements give these people the motive and opportunity. But these crimes are fully preventable.

rConstitution Paper 8

Laws That Exceed Enumerated Powers Are Unconstitutional

CONGRESSMEN IN PRIOR PARTIES have passed, and have left in place, so-called laws that exceed the enumerated powers, in defiance of the Constitution. Presidents in prior parties have signed and executed, and have continued to execute, so-called laws that exceed the enumerated powers, in defiance of the Constitution.[8.1]

The people and the states delegated scope to the national government. All in all, the national-government scope is small.

The Constitution specifies the scope of the national government primarily in Article I,

Section 8 and secondarily elsewhere. The full government scope specified by the Constitution is summarized in Table 8.1 below.

Table 8.1. Constitutional scope[8.2]

Scope item (Opportunity)	Clause	Type (1=Lead, 2=Offset)			
		States	Nation		
			Legislative	Executive	Judicial
Scope not delegated to USA and not prohibited to states	10	1			
Political scope					
Law-of-nations offences	I.8.10		1		
Treaty advice, consent	**II.2.2**		1		
Treaty making	II.2.2			2	
War declaration; marque, reprisal, capture rules	**I.8.11**		1		
Army raising and support up to 2 years	I.8.12		1		
Navy provision and maintenance	I.8.13		1		
Land- and naval-force rules	**I.8.14**		1		
Militia-calling provisions	I.8.15		1		
Militia rules for USA service	I.8.16		1		
Limited government- and military-district laws	I.8.17		1		
Habeas corpus suspension	I.9.2		1		
Treason punishment	III.3.2		1		
Army, Navy, Militia command	II.2.1			2	
Territory laws	IV.3.2		1		
Consent to foreign gifts	I.9.8		1		
Reprieves, pardons except on impeachment	II.2.1			2	

Laws That Exceed Powers

Scope item (Opportunity)	Clause	Type (1=Lead, 2=Offset)			
		States	Nation		
		Legislative	Legislative	Executive	Judicial
Commercial scope					
Commerce regulations	I.8.3		1		
Bankruptcy laws	I.8.4		1		
Money coinage and valuation	**I.8.5**		**1**		
Weights and measures standards	I.8.5		1		
Counterfeiting punishments	I.8.6		1		
Post offices and post roads	I.8.7		1		
Limited exclusive rights for inventors, authors	**I.8.8**		**1**		
Liquor-transport or -import laws	21.2	1			
Support scope					
Naturalization rules	**I.8.4**		**1**		
Voting laws	**15.2**		**1**		
Voting-tax prohibition laws	24.2		1		
Taxes, duties, imposts, excises	I.8.1		1		
Income-tax laws	16		1		
Borrowing on credit of USA	I.8.2		1		
Slavery, involuntary-servitude laws	13.2		1		
Cases under Constitution, USA laws, treaties	III.2.1				2
Cases on ambassadors, ministers, consuls	III.2.1				2
Cases of admiralty and maritime	III.2.1				2
Controversies involving USA	III.2.1				2
Controversies between states, nations, their people	III.2.1				2

8.3

Political, Commercial, and Support Scope

Many of the scope items in Table 8.1 have to do with preventing or fighting war. Legislative people advise and consent on treaties that could lead to war. Legislative people declare war, fund war, and make all rules for war, which plainly includes rules of engagement. The commander in chief commands the people defending against attacks and fighting legislatively-declared wars, following legislatively-determined rules.

Other scope items in Table 8.1 include a very-small number of commerce activities: assure the free flow of goods and services across state lines, govern bankruptcy, coin money and set its value, provide limited exclusive rights for inventors and authors.

Rounding out Table 8.1 are a very-small number of support activities: control naturalization, tax and borrow, judge cases and controversies.[2]

Look closer at Table 8.1, and it's clear that even very-small details are tied down. The Constitution itemizes scope items as specific and narrow as post offices and post roads, and limited exclusive rights for inventors and authors. These are precise, cautious delegations of scope to the national government from the people.

Laws That Exceed Powers

To get these cautious delegations of scope ratified, the proportion of states that needed to approve was a minimum of 69%. To get further delegations of scope ratified, the proportion of states that need to approve is a minimum of 75%.[8.3] Such careful political balancing acts aren't achieved easily or often.

Clearly the states didn't ratify the rigorously-enumerated and rigorously-limited national powers in the Constitution only to have short, general phrases delegate to the national government broad scope to control such things as foods and drugs, health insurance, healthcare cartels, retirement, welfare, energy, labor cartels, pollutants, car and truck requirements, agriculture, communications, education, nationalized lands and parks, and much more.[8.4] But almost anything can get falsely rationalized.

False Rationalizations

The most commonly-used false rationalizations hijack a few brief phrases in the Constitution. Here are those phrases and their actual meanings:
- The scope *"provide for ... the ... general welfare"* means that the only scope delegated by the people to the national government

8.5

is scope that provides for the "general" welfare of all regions and states; no scope is delegated to provide for the special welfare of particular regions or states.[8.5, 8.6]

- The scope *"to regulate Commerce"*[8.7] means the scope to facilitate commerce by specifying certain limited rules: rules to standardize trade of products between people of one state and people of another state, rules to remove obstructions to domestic trade erected by states, and rules to standardize and restrict trade of products between people of the USA and people of other nations and of Indian tribes.[8.8]

- The scope *"To make all Laws necessary and proper for carrying into execution the foregoing powers, and all other Powers vested by this Constitution"*[8.9] means the scope to make incidental laws within the boundaries defined by the enumerated powers. These boundaries are enumerated above this phrase in Article I, Section 8, and also in a few other scattered locations in the Constitution as noted in Table 8.1. Each of these incidental laws is to be made faithfully, carefully, impartially, and representatively.[8.10]

Laws That Exceed Powers

The actual meanings above are the plain public meanings at the time of ratification. These are the only meanings that make sense, considering that specific delegated powers were carefully enumerated. And these are the only meanings that make sense in the context of the historical events that preceded the development of the Constitution.

USA Created to End Scope Creep

The United States of America originated as resourceful settlements, then colonies, and finally states. While taxes as a percentage of gross domestic product for Great Britain's people were almost 20%, taxes for the colonists were just 1% to 2%.[8.11] When England's parliament took the first steps towards subjugating the colonists, the colonists raised armies and declared independence against the strongest army and navy the world had ever seen. The United States people won the war and their independence. Unsurprisingly, these fiercely-independent people's Articles of Confederation delegated very-little power to the national government, authorized national laws and treaties only if the proportion of states that approved was at least 69%, and authorized national amendments only if the proportion of states that approved

8.7

was 100%. Later, to get the Constitution ratified, the proportion of states that needed to approve was again a minimum of 69%. These resolutely-independent people's states absolutely did not ratify a Constitution that delegated diffuse powers to a national government, which would have empowered the national government to subjugate the people.

Rationalizations that the Constitution delegates broad unenumerated powers to the national government run exactly counter to the nature of these people, as demonstrated by these people's many economic, military, and political actions.

It is a wonderful heritage to have this liberty-securing supreme law already in place, ready to be followed.

When government people secure the scope boundaries that the Constitution places on government people, our individual liberty will be maximized, and our rights to life, liberty, and property will be secure.

rConstitution Paper 9
Abortion Is Illegal

CONGRESSMEN IN PRIOR PARTIES *have passed, and have left in place, so-called laws that permit and fund abortions, in defiance of the Declaration and the Constitution.*

Presidents in prior parties have signed and executed, and have continued to execute, so-called laws that permit and fund abortions, in defiance of the Declaration and the Constitution.

State congressmen in prior parties have passed, and have left in place, so-called laws that permit and fund abortions, in defiance of the Declaration and the Constitution.

Governors and state attorneys general in prior parties have signed and executed, and have continued to execute, so-called laws that permit and fund abortions, in defiance of the Declaration and the Constitution.

> *State judges have complied with so-called laws that permit and fund abortions, in defiance of the Declaration and the Constitution.*[9.1]

Abortion is regularly perpetrated without prosecution. This is enabled when people talk about abortion in abstract terms. We will not talk about abortion in abstract terms here. Here, we will focus on evidence.

Unborn Babies Are Alive

From the dawn of recorded history, Jewish people described babies who were not yet born as infants, babies, children, sons.

Four thousand years ago, the author of Job wrote:

> *Or why was I not hidden like a miscarried child,*
> *like infants who never see daylight?*[9.2]

Three thousand five hundred years ago, Moses wrote:

> *… Rebekah conceived. But the children inside her struggled with each other …*[9.3]

Three thousand years ago, David wrote:

> *… you knit me together in my mother's womb.*[9.4]

Abortion

Two thousand years ago, Luke wrote:
> *And consider your relative Elizabeth—even she has conceived a son in her old age, and this is the sixth month for her who was called childless.*[9.5]
> *When Elizabeth heard Mary's greeting, the baby leaped inside her ...*[9.6]

Sixty years ago, newspapers treated abortion as murder.[9.7]

Now, as always, parents who are expecting a baby describe their unborn baby as a baby from the start.

When an egg and a sperm bind together, in less than a second the two cells fuse and form a single cell. A new life begins: The single cell has a unique set of chromosomes, and the cell can develop into a complete organism.

Within the first 1 to 3 minutes of life, changes in calcium start modifying the cell's surface. Before, the egg was receptive to sperm; afterwards, the new life defends itself against binding by additional sperm.

By 30 hours of life, the new cell divides into two cells. Already each cell is biased to develop into different components of the new life's support structure in the womb and of the new life's body.

9.3

By 3 days of life, at 8 to 16 cells, the new life compacts into a solid ball. The outer layer of cells will support development in the womb, while the inner mass of cells will mostly develop into the new body.

At 4 or 5 days of life, the new life is released from its protective protein coat. The outer cells attach to the uterus and form the placenta that transports nutrients and oxygen from the mother to the inner cells that form the body. The outer cells also form membranes that provide a protective environment for the body.[9.8]

Simultaneous Contraception Prevents Conception

Conception and implantation don't happen every ovulatory cycle, but the average probability per cycle can be back-calculated to be about 0.136, given that the average percentage of sexually-active women who would become pregnant in one year with about 13 ovulatory cycles is about 85%.[9.9]

$$1 - (1 - 0.136)^{13}$$
$$= 0.85$$
$$= 17 \; pregnancies \; in \; 20 \; women \; in \; one \; year$$

By tracking fertility using menstruation dates and body temperature, conception and implantation

Abortion

can be reduced from the baseline level when not tracking fertility, 85 pregnancies per 100 woman-years, down to just 1.0 pregnancy per 100 woman-years.[9.10] The average probability of conception and implantation per cycle is reduced by a factor of 0.00566. Over a woman's reproductive lifetime of about 400 cycles,[9.11] the lifetime chance of an unplanned pregnancy becomes about 1/4:

$$1 - \left(1 - 0.136 \cdot \frac{\frac{1.0}{100} \cdot \frac{1}{13}}{0.136}\right)^{400}$$
$$= 1 - (1 - 0.136 \cdot 0.00566)^{400}$$
$$= 0.27$$
$$\cong \frac{1}{4} \text{ chance of an unplanned pregnancy in a lifetime}$$

By also using a combined oral contraceptive that's chosen to reduce ovulation, conception can be reduced further. With 75 µg/kg gestodene (GSD) and 20 µg/kg ethinylestradiol (EE), for example, ovulation was not detected in any of the studies that were reviewed.[9.12] With a 24-day/4-day treatment regimen, ovulation likelihood is reduced even further.[9.13, 9.14]

Unfortunately, the pill's further contraceptive action of thickening cervical mucus to block sperm does little or nothing when it's needed most.[9.14]

Even so, by tracking fertility and by also reducing ovulation using a suitable pill, conception can be made very unlikely.

This means that the pill's other action of preventing implantation never has a chance to come into play.

Since the available studies aren't large enough to characterize the reduced ovulation rate, the reduced ovulation rate must be inferred from the reduced pregnancy rate. Using this rate as shown in the calculation below, the average probability of conception is reduced by a factor of 0.00170.[9.15]

So then by tracking fertility and by also reducing ovulation using a suitable pill, the lifetime chance of an unplanned pregnancy can be reduced to just one in 2,000 lifetimes:

$$1 - \left(1 - 0.136 \cdot 0.00566 \cdot \frac{\frac{0.003}{1} \cdot \frac{1}{13}}{0.136}\right)^{400}$$

$$= 1 - \left(1 - 0.136 \cdot 0.00566 \cdot \frac{0.000231}{0.136}\right)^{400}$$

$$= 1 - (1 - 0.136 \cdot 0.00566 \cdot 0.00170)^{400}$$

$$= 0.00052$$

$$= 1 \text{ unplanned pregnancy in 2,000 lifetimes}$$

This chance may look much lower than needed, but it's the practical result of a practical choice: between using more than one method and using just one method.

Using just one method, the lifetime chance of an unplanned pregnancy starts out unpromisingly high: one out of four.

This chance increases quickly when people have less-than-perfect knowledge, risks, and behavior. People generally don't know how an added risk that sounds small will compound over time into an overall risk that's much larger.[9.16] People who are younger are much-more fertile: their chance of pregnancy in one cycle is 30%;[9.17] their chance of pregnancy in two cycles is 51%. People who are younger also generally are much-less careful.[9.18, 9.19]

If people make the practical choice to use more than one contraception method simultaneously, this creates further options. For example, they can then choose to use male condoms on days when a woman is predicted to be fertile, so there are fewer days they need to abstain from sex, so it's easier to achieve good results.

Good results are especially important here. An unplanned conception is a new life, whose right to life needs to be secure.

An Abortion Comes after Many Choices

A new life is ended by abortion.

Most abortions are surgical. Compared to using medications, surgery is quicker and is more likely to fully expel all the baby's body parts and all the baby's placenta. Painkillers are given to the mother, not to the baby.[9.20] Lethal injections—killing the baby before removing the body—are used sometimes on larger babies: to protect abortion providers from possible penalties for delivering a live baby, or to help the mother and the abortion providers feel better about their experiences.[9.21]

The ways that various babies are treated can evoke strong emotions. But as wrenching as these emotions can feel, these temporary treatments are incidental, in the end.

In the end, what matters is that every abortion ends a life.

Before an abortion, the baby's fate is determined by the individual choices made by many people. The last defense, and least informed, is the mother.

The mother operates, as we all do, by assimilating patterns in the experiences and learning and valuations that she has been presented with up to this point in her life, and by using this assimilated information as the basis for making predictive extrapolations.[9.22] If she's younger, she's unprepared to imagine the full range of possibilities that could unfold for her in her future. An abortion seems best. Then life will go on as she imagines it given her limited understanding.

But afterwards, she continues adding experiences and learning and valuations. She likely marries, she raises children. School plans and early career plans unfold, and they don't turn out just as she had imagined. Her perspective changes. Everyone's does. She finds that she can imagine entirely different options for herself if she had not aborted what she now understands more fully was her child, and if she had instead let her child live with her or with adoptive parents. Likely she accepts, at least eventually, that she made the best decision she could have understood at the time. She can't see how she would have understood differently back then. But why? What had she learned up to that point? Who all had influenced her decision to choose abortion for her baby?

Her baby had a father. She and the father had parents, siblings, extended families. Family relationships have unmatched potential to offer economic and social support. Still, how prepared can any young mother and father be to understand and appreciate how resiliently people can adapt and grow as circumstances change throughout their lives? Parents' and grandparents' lives remain largely mysteries until children begin living adult lives themselves. If young people have ever discussed abortion in their families of origin, how many of those discussions even began to realistically contemplate how life could be replanned and lived well given a child? Or how adoption might work? There are better possibilities than most young mothers and fathers can imagine and choose.

One major change in modern life has been that in our early years we are less frequently confronted with death, so these circumstances that had naturally drawn most people to religious faith in the past no longer draw most people to religious faith now. The church and religious faith have become, for many people, not natural core experiences in people's earlier years but, instead, adjunct experiences that eventually deepen as people become more mature in later years as adults. The church and religious faith are naturally put off until after people finally wring enough useful skills out of their schooling and finally begin to be able to earn a living in the modern world, marry, and begin families.[9.23, 9.24] Early marriage, although encouraged by some faiths since sexuality is naturally tempting, becomes economically difficult.[9.25] Siblings lost to childhood diseases, family members and neighbors dying in wars, fathers and mothers dying in middle age from heart attacks and breast cancer—these are mostly not our experiences now. What, then, are our experiences now? What is our learning?

Education has become, now more than ever, a delay in our ability to earn a living, a delay that is ever-lengthening—and decoupled from performance—simply because this status quo can be kept in place by a political equilibrium. Teachers largely vote in the Democratic Party bloc to maintain government-monopoly schools and teachers' unions. Government-monopoly schools and unionized teachers in turn produce students who vote in the same bloc. This voting continues until the students' early school experience and learning get enriched and challenged by later experiences in businesses, in which, in most cases, they learn to add value—not value that people are coerced by government people to pay for indirectly through taxes, but rather value that people choose to pay for directly themselves. Education substantially delays integration into the larger world of human activities and potential. This strongly delays young people's development of the ability, when needed, to visualize possibilities other than abortion.

9.11

Secondarily, current educational experiences limit young people's understanding of how to use contraceptives. Having spent most of their early years in the care of and under the heavy influence of teachers, people of childbearing age in the USA create unplanned pregnancies at a rate of 3.4 million a year. Failures to use contraceptives are primary causes of the unplanned pregnancies at a rate of 1.8 million a year. Failures to use contraceptives consistently are primary causes of the unplanned pregnancies at a rate of 1.4 million a year.[9.26] Such rates require high levels of basic ignorance of available medications and techniques, and high levels of basic ignorance of the relevant statistics.

Further, current educational experiences increase the separation of young people from families, increase the modern separation of young people from religious understanding, and inculcate an undeserved respect for government decisions and activities.

Current educational experiences, then, have the net effects that young people are more likely to become pregnant, and young people are more likely to choose abortion.

Abortion also is made more likely by entertainment media and advertising. Sex sells. Sex is everywhere. Abortion, when mentioned, is framed as a

Abortion

choice, so that abortion is freedom; and freedom, of course, is a core American dream. Movies routinely resolve major dramatic themes within at most three hours; TV sitcoms routinely resolve situations within airtimes of 23 minutes.[9.27] Abortion increasingly is presented like a similar magic solution.[9.28]

Abortion is presented as a solution—as a right—more directly by counselors, social workers, and medical workers.[9.29] The fraction of practicing obstetrician-gynecologists who perpetrate abortions is small, 14%.[9.30] Even so, the fraction of all physicians who believe that physicians are obligated to present abortion as a choice if contraception has failed is large, 86%.[9.31] In 1847 the brand-new American Medical Association prioritized making abortion illegal;[9.32] but in 1970 the AMA chose to support doctors who choose to perpetrate abortion on request, wherever abortion is said to be legal.[9.33]

So what's deceptively framed as the mother's choice is really the product of a cascade of choices, essentially all of which are choices made by people who, compared to the mother, are much, much better informed. This cascade of choices ends with the choices of the medical workers, preceded by the choices of the poorly-informed mother, the poorly-informed father, the families, the counselors, the social workers, the religious people, the teachers, the advertising people, and the entertainment media people. Furthest upstream, and the most influential, are the choices of the people who determine the general belief that abortion is legal.

The general belief that abortion is legal is incorrect.

Rights Are Mostly Secured by Structure

The Declaration of Independence lists life as the first right that is to be secured by government:

> *... all men are created equal ... they are endowed by their Creator with certain unalienable Rights ... among these are Life, Liberty and the pursuit of Happiness ... to secure these rights, Governments are instituted among Men ...*[9.34]

The strongest ways that the Constitution secures individual rights are through structural protections: limited enumerated government scopes, separated powers, and above all, offsetting powers.

The worst excesses that can be committed against other individuals are the excesses that are committed by people as a group. The most-lethal groups of people anywhere are the people

Abortion

empowered by governments. The USA government gets limited most strongly when people in national and state governments exercise their constitutional powers against other people in national and state governments. This need for structural protection, together with the strength of these structural protections, is why the structural protections in the Constitution are the strongest-possible protections for individual rights.

Interestingly, this structure is designed to not provide many deadly-serious protections for rights through action at the national level, but to instead provide these deadly-serious protections through action at the state level. Murder, for instance, deprives an individual of his or her most-fundamental right: the right to life; and yet murder is not covered by any scope enumerated in the Constitution for the national government. This scope was reserved to the states and is taken care of by each state. In each state, murder is illegal, so the national government doesn't need laws on murder.

The national government similarly doesn't need to act on a wide range of policy issues (even though Progressives in the national government do regularly violate the national government's constitutional boundaries). The Constitution's structural protections are acceptable for nearly every policy issue, and are particularly successful for criminalizing various serious actions.

Liberty Needed Support

Historically, structural protections failed on one serious policy issue: slavery. People in the wealthy, large region that treated slavery as legal and people in the less-wealthy, smaller region that acknowledged slavery as criminal formed a military and trade alliance, the United States of America, to win and maintain independence.[9.35] People saw the alliance as essential for survival as mostly free people. Ben Franklin depicted the colonies as a snake severed into provinces, a vivid embodiment of the caption's message "JOIN, or DIE."[9.36]

From the start of the original alliance, and for the duration, the Declaration of Independence's principle was codified into the Constitution, making slavery illegal:

> *This Constitution, and the Laws of the United States which shall be made in Pursuance thereof ... shall be the supreme Law of the Land ... any Thing in the Constitution or Laws of any State to the Contrary notwithstanding.*[9.37]

Abortion

> *No person shall ... be deprived of life, liberty, or property, without due process of law ...*[9.38]
>
> *... [the president] shall take the following Oath or Affirmation: — "I do solemnly swear (or affirm) that I will faithfully execute the Office of President of the United States, and will to the best of my Ability, preserve, protect and defend the Constitution of the United States."*[9.39]
>
> *The Senators and Representatives before mentioned, and the Members of the several State Legislatures, and all executive and judicial Officers, both of the United States and of the several States, shall be bound by Oath or Affirmation, to support this Constitution ...*[9.40]

So the Constitution governs, life and liberty and property are protected, and national and state officers are conscience-bound to support the Constitution. National and state officers are each individually empowered and mandated to not pass laws, execute laws, or opine for laws that don't protect life and liberty and property.

In this way, the Constitution's primary structural protection of all rights, enumerated or

9.17

unenumerated, is backstopped by secondary rights protection of a limited number of rights explicitly covered in the Constitution.

During the period when people in the USA perpetrated slavery, the Constitution's protection of liberty was not acted on either by people in the national government or by people in the state governments in the wealthy, large region where people treated slavery as legal.

It's not clear how long the original military and trade alliance that allowed slavery was needed for survival. Military alliances are insurance. When a military alliance prevents loss, the need and the cost can in retrospect look like more than was needed for the whole time. Here, the original alliance held for more than 80 years.

In this time, people in the region that acknowledged slavery as criminal increasingly industrialized, growing more efficient and wealthier. Meanwhile, people in the region that treated slavery as legal continued their primarily labor-intensive farming activities, growing more slowly and becoming relatively-less powerful. From 1774 to 1860, the fraction of total personal income in all thirteen colonies or states that was earned in the slavery-treated-as-legal region declined from 57% to 31%.[9.41, 9.1] This period finally was ended by secession.

Abortion

Secession, and the war that followed, exiled the people who supported slavery. This finally broke the original alliance so that the Constitution's protection of liberty finally could be supported. During wartime when the region that acknowledged slavery as criminal held all the national-government power, their people began codifying further law reinforcing that slavery is illegal. This culminated in:

> No State shall ... deprive any person of life, liberty, or property, without due process of law ...[9.42]

This new law let the government people save face. They could still pretend that prior law didn't outlaw slavery, and they could now say that current law did outlaw slavery.

The new law acted chiefly by simply establishing a turning point. Once the new law passed, the government people began supporting the existing law that slavery was illegal.

Life Needs Support

Unlike with slavery, with abortion there are structural protections in place universally in every state. A baby who has not yet been born is alive. The baby's life is ended by abortion. Abortion is murder. Murder is illegal in every state.

Like with slavery, there are rights protections in place. Plus unlike back when slavery was perpetrated, these rights protections have now been further reinforced by the same amendment that reinforced that slavery was criminal. The resulting rights-protection supreme law is worth restating in full:

> *This Constitution, and the Laws of the United States which shall be made in Pursuance thereof … shall be the supreme Law of the Land … any Thing in the Constitution or Laws of any State to the Contrary notwithstanding.*[9.37]
>
> *No person shall … be deprived of life, liberty, or property, without due process of law …*[9.38]
>
> *No State shall … deprive any person of life, liberty, or property, without due process of law …*[9.42]
>
> *… [the president] shall take the following Oath or Affirmation: — "I do solemnly swear (or affirm) that I will faithfully execute the Office of President of the United States, and will to the best of my Ability, preserve, protect and defend the Constitution of the United States."*[9.39]

Abortion

The Senators and Representatives before mentioned, and the Members of the several State Legislatures, and all executive and judicial Officers, both of the United States and of the several States, shall be bound by Oath or Affirmation, to support this Constitution ...[9.40]

Both structural protections and rights protections have been failing on this second serious policy issue of abortion. The problem, as with slavery, is an enduring political equilibrium state that allows people to not follow the Constitution.

But the equilibrium state on abortion can more quickly be shattered. With slavery, the political equilibrium was initially necessary to create a nation large enough to survive, and the political equilibrium was sustained by economic strength that changed slowly. With abortion, the political equilibrium is not necessary to ensure that the nation survives, and the political equilibrium is sustained by political dynamics that can be changed rapidly.

Perpetuation of abortion, and nonsupport of the Constitution's structural and rights protections for life, is helped along by specialization in politics. In modern life, politicians need specialized skills to look good in the media and to speak articulately. Given those skills, politicians have most of what they need to continue in office, and they have less need to perform well in office. Often, government people's understanding of the government comes primarily from what they learn on the job once they're elected. People learn quite a lot by example. In the predominant work activity elsewhere in life—working in businesses adding value—good results matter, so the examples provided by other people who have more experience are good. Unfortunately in government, the examples provided by other people who have more experience have long been bad. These examples teach government people how to not follow the Constitution.

Progressives, who don't follow the Constitution, have controlled our national and state governments, with only temporary, partial pauses, for well over a century.[9.43] Progressive supermajorities of elected representatives don't follow the Constitution, and Progressive supermajorities of appointed officials don't follow the Constitution. The root cause is that Progressives dominate both major parties.[9.44]

This domination is maintained through party rules. The parties have no purity tests for

Abortion

candidates. The parties sanction debates hosted and controlled by Progressive media people. The parties allow primaries rather than caucuses, early selection contests in states where the party is relatively weak, open contests, winner-take-all or winner-take-most contests, party electors from regions that send no presidential electors, and multiple contests on the same day.[9.1] Party rules enable party executives to gather substantial funds, and empower party executives to prop up candidates who party voters don't like and to attack candidates who party voters do like.

Fortunately, though, parties can't stop government people from taking the first substantial independent steps to support the existing rights-protection regime. In the national government and in the state governments, each executive, legislative, and judicial official is independently accountable for protecting or supporting the Constitution.

State attorneys general should summarily announce that from this day forward they will not support the Supreme Court's unconstitutional opinions on abortion and they will support the Constitution's protection of life, so any abortion perpetrated from this day forward will be prosecuted as murder. Governors and presidents should announce that murder convictions for abortion will be enforced fully, and any appeals opinions that use unconstitutional arguments will not be enforced. State and national legislators should meet in emergency sessions to immediately end state funding for abortions; otherwise, if these people don't, they should face state prosecutions as abortion perpetrators.

Abortion perpetrators likely will hold out in political strongholds in some states. Further measures should be taken against these people, starting with those states' attorneys general, who effectively will be perpetrating abortions that are murders. USA attorneys should summarily announce that from this day forward they will not support the Supreme Court's unconstitutional opinions on abortion and they will support the Constitution's protection of life, so any abortion perpetrated from this day forward in these states will be prosecuted in national courts under the applicable state's law on murder. Representatives and senators should summarily impeach and convict every national judge or justice who refuses to convict abortion perpetrators for murder. Presidents and senators should replace each such abortion-perpetrating judge or justice with a judge or justice who agrees to allow abortion perpetrators to be convicted for murder. USA attorneys should follow by prosecuting each such abortion-perpetrating judge or justice.

Life Will Win Out in the End

It's important to know from the outset that the actions of people who don't support the Constitution are the responsibility of those people alone. The officer of a state or national government is empowered only to do the right thing himself and let the chips fall where they may.

Will this bring change? How quickly?

Change can come in many possible ways, and extremely quickly.

Every single abortion comes only after many choices: ill-informed choices of the unborn baby's mother and father, possibly choices of counselors, choices of medical workers, choices of multiple government people. Immediately when some government officers begin to support the Constitution, each of the choices of other people about abortion will no longer appear clearly protected by unconstitutional Supreme Court opinions and by unconstitutional actions and inactions of other people in national and state governments. Some of the people making choices about abortion will no longer believe with full certainty that abortion is legal; and given this change, these people will choose from that day forward to not conspire to perpetrate an abortion, committing a murder. Maybe most of these people will quickly choose to not be a part of abortion and murder. Conceivably all key people, once newly faced with choosing directly and facing consequences, could quickly choose to not be a part of abortion and murder. Most Americans respect the rule of law highly; all people consider what's in their own best interests.

People in political strongholds could keep choosing to conspire to perpetrate abortions, committing murder. Judges on trials or on appeals could rule unconstitutionally. Impeachment convictions would require senators to vote for conviction with supermajorities of 2/3.

This threshold could be reached quickly, without elections, if sitting senators, when called to cast their first votes on the record, choose to vote in favor of protecting life as required by the Constitution. This threshold could be reached within 2 years if the proportion of senators replaced approaches 1/3, and if the remaining senators see their elections nearing and, in self-interest, choose to change their votes to favor protecting life as required by the Constitution.

This threshold could be reached within 6 years if new senators are repeatedly elected.

This threshold could approach and recede and approach again over a longer timescale, as the balance of power between the existing Progressive parties shifts.

This threshold could be crossed very rapidly if a new party is formed whose candidates support the Constitution once in office. Such candidates have been the most-electable ever: Washington and Reagan exceeded all other candidates with their all-time-highest first-term electoral percentages.[9.45]

When stability is maintained by defying the law, stability is bad. Stability means that the law is defied in all places and the law is likely to continue to be defied in all places in the future.

When instability results from obeying the law, instability is good.

Instability means that the law is obeyed in some places. In the securing of liberty from slavery, instability meant that through emancipation, the securing of liberty first took place in some places in the South that were controlled by the North. In the securing of life from abortion, instability would similarly mean that the securing of life would first take place in some places where state-government

9.27

people would lead in following the Constitution. Securing liberty in at least some place or securing life in at least some place is clearly good.

Instability also means that the law is likely to be obeyed in all places more quickly.

Once slaves had refuges to which they could flee in some places, this made it possible for slaves to succeed at escaping from slavery in other places. This made slavery less viable in other places. As a result, this helped make the securing of liberty more quickly spread to all places. In Brazil, this was the primary process by which slaves became free (and without war, the same as in most nations).[9.46]

Securing of life would proceed differently, but instability would still help the process proceed more quickly. The securing of life from abortion in some places would help people understand that the Constitution secures life from abortion in all places. The securing of life from abortion in some places would also immediately kick-start further development of support infrastructure to help prevent pregnancies and assist with pregnancies in those places. Additional visible changes in attitudes and in practices would surely follow. All these changes would make the securing of life start to be seen as inevitable in all places. This would make the securing of life start to spread to all places.

In a battle between quick change to a good policy and quick change to a bad policy, quick change to a good policy will work better, and will win in the end.[9.47] But the battle must start, and must continue. People in government must be determined to change to good policies by fully using their constitutional powers.

In the example scenarios above, people who support the Constitution would start fully using their constitutional powers to support the Constitution. Compared to giving speeches, compared to taking partial actions that affirm the remaining status quo, compared to taking no decisive actions—this would be a sea change. Compared to secession, this would be a measured response. Compared to industrial war on a region's nongovernment people, this would be a moral response.

When the issue was slavery, the social arrangement had stretched back into prehistory, and the relative economic strength had started out substantial and had held for over 80 years.

When the issue is abortion, the root cause is a political calculation by Progressives, enabled by Progressives' dominance in both major parties.

Progressive dominance is nearly as strong at the state level, since people at the state level vie to run for national offices. Progressives dominate schools, media, medicine, the legal profession. Progressives' perpetration of abortion has held for over 40 years.

But appearances deceive. Abortion support is a house of cards. Given forceful, direct pushback, the citadel's facade will flatten, and past perpetrators will see life differently.

Simultaneous contraception prevents conception. Unborn babies are alive. Murder is illegal. By the Constitution's rights protections and the states' laws on murder, abortion is illegal. By the Constitution's structural protections, abortion can be opposed using decisive constitutional powers of individual state and national-government people who individually support the Constitution.

This is the way the Constitution is designed to secure the right to life.

rConstitution Paper 10

Fractional-Reserve Banking Is Unconstitutional

CONGRESSMEN IN PRIOR PARTIES *have passed, and have left in place, so-called laws authorizing fractional-reserve banking, paper money not backed 100% by gold or silver, and a central bank, in defiance of the Declaration and the Constitution.*

Presidents in prior parties have signed and executed, and have continued to execute, so-called laws authorizing fractional-reserve banking, paper money not backed 100% by gold or silver, and a central bank, in defiance of the Declaration and the Constitution.[10.1]

Good Money Matters

On July 4, 1840, President Martin Van Buren signed "the second declaration of independence,"[10.2] this time independence from unredeemable paper money that caused crises such as in 1837 and 1839.[10.3]

Under his predecessor President Andrew Jackson, the national government already no longer chartered banks. This had eliminated a major nationwide source of inflation and instability.[10.4]

Now the national government would only use gold or silver money, or bank money that banks promised to redeem with gold or silver from reserves worth only a fraction of the money's face value.[10.2] Gold or silver backing would eliminate paper money inflation and would further reduce instability. Reserves that were only fractional, though, would still add instability.

Next, these initial Democrats' program called for making the state governments also no longer charter banks. This would eliminate government people's favor of letting their crony bank people hold less than 100% reserves.[10.4] Eliminating the use of fractional reserves would eliminate instability due to government money error.

In advancing this program, in steering clear of potential wars on both borders, and in confronting financial crises in 1837 and 1839 by helpfully

Fractional-Reserve Banking

reducing government spending, President Van Buren did the right thing and let the chips fall as they may.

The hammer did fall, soon. The financial crises in 1837 and 1839, the averted wars to expand the nation northward and southward, and hyped concerns that the new Democratic party was becoming an autocracy all combined to swell turnout and produce a strong defeat of President Van Buren in his bid for a second term. Even so, President Van Buren's well-executed single term produced a legacy that was second to none.

President Van Buren's refusal to bail out state governments prevented future state-government extravagances that would have recreated a major contributing cause of the financial crisis of 1839.[10.2] His noninterference at the start of the 4-year crisis, during which prices fell by a massive 46%,[10.5] established a pattern of noninterference that left people in business free to adjust quickly. People did start adjusting quickly from the start, and adjusting well. Those 4 years, real GNP didn't even fall, but instead rose 16%. In striking contrast starting with the stock-market crash in 1929, in the following 4-year period during which prices fell by a smaller 31%, and continuing long afterward, President Herbert Hoover and President Franklin

Roosevelt established a pattern of complex, strong interference that left people in business unable to react effectively. Those first 4 years, real GNP fell 30%;[10.6] and for more than a decade, real GNP stagnated—the Great Depression.

By doing the right thing in many instances—following principles now called classical liberal, and libertarian[10.7]—President Van Buren shaped the early Democratic Party people into the strongest protectors of economic liberty anywhere. Compared to the people of any other nation, Americans enjoyed greater freedom from government intervention until almost the century's end. As a result in this period, despite the Civil War's massive destruction, America developed mightily.[10.2]

What was it back then that made voters and a major political party attach prime importance to money, which in our modern experience sounds boring, or at least geeky? Are we descended from geeks? No. Rather, unlike people now, people back then still had basic needs that could readily go unsatisfied, so they suffered eye-opening hardships due to bad money.

With bad money, prices sometimes fall significantly, and borrowers lose big. For instance, as mentioned earlier, from February 1839 to February 1843 the wholesale price of a weighted

Fractional-Reserve Banking

load of commodities fell 46%. For a person who borrowed money and spent it when prices were highest, the real value of his loan balance rose 87%. He didn't get any more money to invest, but he ended up owing much more because of how the banking system worked.

And with bad money, prices sometimes rise significantly, and lenders' property is lost. From April 1834 to February 1837 the wholesale price of the same load of commodities rose 52%. For a person who loaned money when prices were lowest, the real value of the loan balance that he would be repaid fell 52%. He ended up worth much less because of how the banking system worked.

These losses occur in cycles whose scale and timing have not been predicted well until very recently,[10.8] but whose operation is well-understood qualitatively.

GME "Gimme" Government Money Error Cycles per Austrian Economics

The natural levels of interest rates are what result from the current levels of saving today. If people save more money today, they will have more money tomorrow to buy more tomorrow. The more money people save today, the lower the natural interest rates will be today.

10.5

When the government people control money, they can and do cause interest rates to be lower than the natural rates. They do this by causing the total stock of money to increase.

When, as a result, interest rates are lower than the natural interest rates, people in business and people in households can borrow money more easily. When people can borrow money more easily than they would have at the natural interest rates that are sustainable, people do borrow and use more money.

When people use more money, people buy stocks and bonds and real estate, inflating stock and bond and real-estate prices.

When people in households use more money, they buy more consumer services and goods, and they overconsume consumer services and goods.

People see stocks and bonds and real estate values that on paper are high, and people in households see salaries that on paper are high, so people also save too little to keep the natural interest rates low, and the natural interest rates become even higher. This change isn't visible in the prevailing interest rates for as long as the government people keep the prevailing interest rates unnaturally low.

People in business see high sales and low prevailing interest rates. People in business see incomes that on paper are high and borrowing costs that on paper are low. People in business therefore spend less now to sustain or upgrade existing capital investments in equipment and plants, and they overconsume their existing capital stock. That is, they malinvest by underinvesting in sustainable businesses.

At the same time, since people in business have incomes that on paper are high and borrowing costs that on paper are low, they also spend more on longer-term and higher-risk ventures. That is, they also malinvest by overinvesting in unsustainable businesses.

Throughout such unnatural booms, government people have a couple of options.

One option for government people is to keep inflating money. This ends very badly.

Having driven savings low and consumption high, and having driven sustainable capital investment low and unsustainable capital investment high, consumer needs and wants are satisfied less well. Eventually, the mistakes pile up and form a critical mass. People respond rationally to this pileup by reassessing their overconsumption. Slowdown comes fast.

By then, savings have been pushed very low, so the natural interest rates have been pushed very high. At very-high interest rates, very-few people in business are able and willing to invest.

Interest rates can only come down when savings are higher. And even when people start saving more, their savings accumulate slowly.

Even worse, in this case the government people keep fighting people's healthy natural reactions, by continuing to do whatever the government people can do to keep interest rates unnaturally low. The government people partially succeed, and this partially suppresses savings.

The result is that after government people have done this enough, eventually recovery comes very slowly at first, and eventually recovery becomes very small.

The other option for government people is to fully stop inflating money. This ends better.

Even so, at first, in the near term, the situations for people in households and for people in business look qualitatively the same as when government people keep inflating money, so this begins badly. Slowdown comes fast.

Low saving and high malinvestment have driven the natural interest rates high, so at first few people in business invest. Recovery comes slowly at first.

But even so, in this case recovery moves along as quickly as possible. The resulting natural interest rates instantly communicate the impact of the

Fractional-Reserve Banking

money people are saving today on how much more money people will have available to spend in the future. People in business are able to take actions that are the best possible, day after day. The natural interest rates do begin to fall, speeding recovery, and the natural interest rates stay lower throughout the recovery.

And in this case, investment and consumption remain sustainable. There are no unnatural interest rates communicating false information. There are no people in government exerting sluggish controls in unnatural cycles in which the money stock is at first quickly inflated and then eventually is slowly inflated or is deflated. With natural interest rates feeding back true information about future prospects, people in business and people in households are able to proceed on optimum trajectories, are able to quickly make optimum corrective actions when natural disasters unfold, and are able to take optimum advantage when positive discoveries and innovations arise.

Whether the government people keep inflating money or the government people eventually stop inflating money, in both cases the principal economic cycle turns out to have been created by the actions of people in government. Unnaturally-low interest rates have brought price inflation.

10.9

Under such top-down misdirection, errors always build up until more-natural (but unnaturally-high) interest rates must be restored.[10.9]

In President Van Buren's time, this restoration was accompanied by severe price deflation. Even so, production continued, and people's material needs kept being met. Plus, back then such restorations were nearly total, and came quickly. The overall trend of natural growth—real growth—was strong and sustained.

More recently, such restorations are less complete, and price inflation usually continues but more slowly. Since usually some top-down misdirection continues, usually some errors continue building up, just more slowly for a while.

Lossy Money Stock

Unnaturally-low interest rates misdirect people.

Mistakes pile up and lead to rapid slowdowns that have serious consequences. People lose jobs, and people in business lose income.

Mistakes plus lowered savings mean that people in business also add less value all of the time, with further consequences. People in households lose out on product quantities, selection, and quality.

Fractional-Reserve Banking

Unnaturally-low interest rates are produced by letting people in banks take deposit money in and promise to return it on demand, but then turn around and loan some of that money out. It's not as if people in banks couldn't make loans without loaning out the same deposit money that they promise to return on demand. People in banks could simply only loan out the money that customers agree the people in banks can use for a while, and keep safe all the money that the people in banks promise to return on demand. People in business would still invest. But in this case, they would invest loan money that has been knowingly committed to their use for a while.

Also, people in business would invest by sharing partial ownership of their business by selling shares of common stock. Partial ownership much more-effectively shares the risks, and much more-effectively shares the rewards. This is good business.

The power to take demand-deposit money and loan some of it out is power that people in banks are granted by people in governments. People in governments charter banks, and people in governments sometimes declare that people in banks don't have to return people's demand-deposit money right away.

10.11

In President Van Buren's time, people in banks issued their own banknotes and decided for themselves what fraction of gold deposits they would keep safe and not lend out: what fraction they would keep in reserve. Now, people in the national government decide what fraction of paper-money deposits that bankers must keep in reserve. The fractions kept in reserve are the banks' fractional reserves.

The smaller the fraction of deposit money that people in banks keep in reserve, the more money they loan out, and the more likely they won't have enough money on hand when people want it back.

In President Van Buren's time and continuing for many years afterward, banks would start failing and those banks' depositors would lose their money. These concentrated property losses got the attention of people in government. Sooner or later, people in government would tell the remaining banks that they didn't have to pay back the money that was deposited for as long as it took until things got better and people's demands eased up.

Now, people in government print the money. When people's demands are high, people in government print much more money and loan it to banks so banks can return people's money.

Fractional-Reserve Banking

Printing more money while the amounts of services and goods available stay the same means that a given amount of money eventually buys fewer services and goods. So people who have any money, and people who have notes that promise future payment of fixed amounts of money, find that eventually a fraction of the value of that money has been taken from them. Savers and lenders lose property.

Borrowers, on the other hand, receive more-valuable money early and repay with less-valuable money later, so borrowers receive windfall markdowns of the real value of their debts. By owing less, borrowers gain property.

The biggest such winners from inflation are the people in government.

People in government keep interest rates down in the near term so that it will cost them less to pay the interest on government debts. This also makes it cost less for them to borrow more, so they can hand out more money and get more votes. On top of the near-term benefits, in the long term when time comes to repay, people in government end up repaying only a portion of the real value that they originally borrowed.

While this stealth tax is a windfall for people in government, it's a loss for all the people who loaned them a fixed amount of money that would not be adjusted for inflation. And while this stealth tax is a windfall for the people who borrowed a fixed amount of money that would not be adjusted for inflation, it's a loss for the people who loaned them the money.

Even if the people in government inflate the stock of money only enough to make prices constant, there are also losses. Without the people in government adding money that inflates the total money stock, the existing money would become more valuable over time. Over time, there are more people, so they produce more services and goods even if productivity is constant. Over time, people on average also become more productive, so they produce even more services and goods. Since over time more and more services and goods get produced, if the money stock would remain constant then the same constant money stock would end up being used to sell and buy more services and goods. Any given product would have to be sold and bought using a smaller portion of the money. So then, any given product's price would have to become less. When the same products can be bought for less money, that means that the money is more valuable.

Fractional-Reserve Banking

This natural price deflation is gradual enough to not cause disruptive large stealth transfers of property from lenders to borrowers. Everyone gets more products and better products for their money, so everyone is relatively better off. When everyone is better off, it's not such a big concern for people when they lose a relatively-small amount of money by borrowing without adjusting for deflation and later repaying an amount that's worth a little more in real terms. Such natural deflation is predictable enough to plan for. Even better, everyone's purchasing power ends up greater overall, so everyone ends up better off overall.

All things considered, natural deflation reflects developments that are good. So when, instead, government people unnaturally hold prices steady, preventing all people who have at least some money from getting the benefit of naturally-good deflation, this is not good. People lose.

Losses of jobs, losses of income, losses of quantities, losses of selection, losses of quality, losses of deposits, losses of savings value, losses of money's naturally-increasing value due to population growth and productivity growth—our money is lossy, because people in government let people

10.15

in banks safeguard only a fraction of deposits: a fractional reserve.

But people in government—in their own actions, or through the actions of their designees, the people in banks—have no power to deprive people of their property without due process of law:

> *No person shall ... be deprived of life, liberty, or property, without due process of law ...* [10.10]

> *No State shall ... deprive any person of life, liberty, or property, without due process of law ...* [10.11]

This means people in government have no power to give amnesty for fraudulent[10.12] banking, and they have no power to inflate money.

Based on property rights alone, then, fractional-reserve banking is unconstitutional. But wait, there's more.

Constant Money Stock

> *The Congress shall have Power ...* [10.13]

> *To coin Money, regulate the Value thereof, and of foreign Coin ...* [10.14]

> *To make all Laws which shall be necessary and proper for carrying into Execution the foregoing Powers ...* [10.15]

10.16

Fractional-Reserve Banking

No State shall ... coin Money; emit Bills of Credit; make any Thing but gold and silver Coin a Tender in Payment of Debts ...[10.16]

The powers not delegated to the United States by the Constitution, nor prohibited by it to the States, are reserved to the States respectively, or to the people.[10.17]

Based on the historical record and on statements made during the Constitutional Convention, during the ratifying conventions, and in the press at the time, the power to coin money does not include the power to print paper money without holding gold or silver in reserve in quantities sufficient to redeem 100% of the paper money's value.[10.18]

The national government is restricted to enumerated powers. The government has no enumerated powers to charter fractional-reserve banking, which would produce instability and inflation. The government has no enumerated powers to charter a central bank, which would direct fractional-reserve banking and inflation. The government has enumerated powers only to mint gold coin and silver coin of regulated weights.

At the time of ratification, this hard money was the state-of-the-art soundest money, and it is required through particularly-rigorous controls. There are rights protections for individual

10.17

property in money. Plus, as preventive measures, these rights protections are explicitly secured by enumerated powers for money control. Through these controls, the Constitution bans people in government from allowing fractional reserves, from allowing paper money not backed 100% by gold or silver, and from running a central bank.

When attempts have been made to define the dollar as one weight of gold and another weight of silver, either gold or silver has eventually turned out to be undervalued. Since the undervalued coins' metal content is worth more than their face values in dollars, the undervalued gold or silver has disappeared from circulation. When one metal disappears from circulation, the total money stock isn't constant, it's deflated.[10.19, 10.20] Prices fall, and borrowers are obligated to pay back more real value than their loans were worth when they signed their contracts. This brings political pressure to allow banks to hold not full reserves of the savings they have on deposit but only fractional reserves, and, using the fractional reserves as a partial safety precaution, to issue an increased total amount of money stock into circulation.[10.20] This is a problematic fix for a problematic result of a problematic initial action.[10.21]

The root cause is that people in Congress don't reassess values rapidly enough to keep both metals in circulation. The dollar simply needs to be defined as a weight of gold only, with silver floating at market rates, or as a weight of silver only, with gold floating at market rates.[10.19]

The resulting hard money is not lossy. It prevents losses of jobs, losses of income, losses of quantities, losses of selection, losses of quality, losses of deposits, losses of savings value, and losses of money's naturally-increasing value due to population growth and due to productivity growth.

The Constitution does not permit the national or state governments to coin money in cryptocurrency.

Cryptocurrency at first looks potentially able to serve as a constant money stock and also offer low storage costs.

But on closer examination, cryptocurrency is missing something elemental. Gold and silver have long been sought as precious metals. This has established a history of discovery, extraction, and refining. Given this history, the total stocks of gold and silver have been reliably shown to naturally remain nearly constant, rising at rates that almost always are slow and that almost always can be easily projected into the near-term future.

Cryptocurrency, on the other hand, is not a precious, long-sought element. It's subject to private politics, government politics,[10.22] counterfeiting, accidental loss, sabotage, and destruction in ways that, given the lack of prior history, are unknowable and unpredictable. Unlike money backed 100% by gold and silver, cryptocurrency can't be trusted to provide a nearly-constant money stock that, compared to fractional-reserve money, is much less lossy.

But another money does offer the same benefits of nearly-constant, predictably-changing money stock, with a better-established historical total stock like gold or silver. It also offers the definitive added benefit of also being inherently productive, and therefore generating added returns not offered by any competing money. This money is productive money.

Productive Money Stock

Common stock is a share in ownership of a company. Companies add more value, and reliably produce greater long-term returns for their owners, than any other thing of value that every individual can own.

This is true in an economy that's initially industrializing, in an economy that's growing to world dominance, and in an economy that's dominant[10.23] but that's also saddled with a large, economic-cycle-inducing government.

A long-time comparison of the growth of major stores of value is shown in Figure 10.1 below. Over the 210-year period shown, the dollar eventually lost value, when the government eventually inflated the money stock, making dollars more lossy. Gold held its value (and, on paper, appeared to gain value when the government inflated the dollar). Government short-term Treasury bills and government long-term bonds paid out more

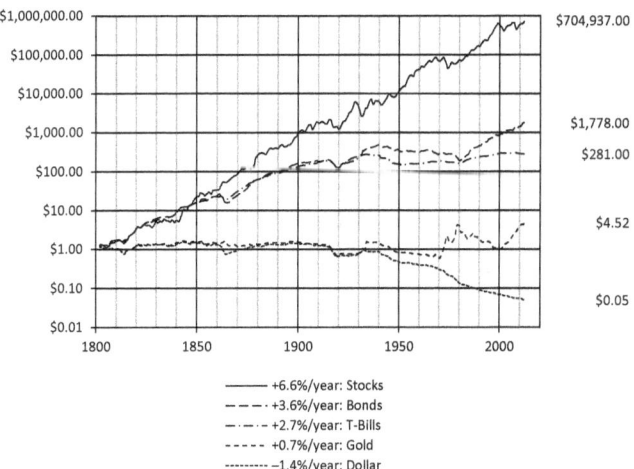

Figure 10.1. Total real returns on USA stocks, government long-term bonds, government short-term Treasury bills, gold, and dollars, 1802–2012 (Data source: McGraw-Hill Education)[10.24]

real value. Common stocks, though, added dramatically-more real value. Common stocks on average added value steadily and exponentially (as shown by the straight line on the figure's semi-log graph, where time on the horizontal axis is scaled linearly, and real value on the vertical axis is scaled exponentially).

The long-term exponential growth in value of common stocks is only what should be expected.

Common stocks are ownership of real assets, real assets that are directly important to people in their daily lives. People use these assets to add value to earn a better living for themselves and their families. When some people have trouble adding value using a company's real assets, these people get replaced by other people who have more success at adding value using the company's real assets. Resources are scarce and can be counted on to get used well, so the values of real assets can be counted on to grow.

When common stocks' real-asset value grows exponentially, this simply means that the more real-asset money you have, the more real-asset money you make.

People in government can and do hold back the amount that this engine adds value, but even so, there's no viable alternative. For creating value

Fractional-Reserve Banking

on a large scale, this engine is the only vehicle around.

Common stock has a bedrock role in the economy. Common stock has massive intrinsic real-asset value. Common stock represents real assets that are going to be owned, so at any given time the underlying real-asset value is constant; issuing more stock certificates can't inflate the real value of the underlying assets. With common stock, 100% of the assets are held in reserve, backing the total of the common stock. Common stock is supported by an incomparable legal knowledge base on how to preserve its property value. Common stock inherently gets adapted by the companies' employees to new opportunities in the evolving economy. Common stock is singularly productive. Given this unique combination of features of common stock, no remotely-comparable alternative store of value exists or will exist to use as money stock.

A common-stock-based monetary system could be readily assembled from proven components that are available now, thanks to recent advancements in computing and communications technology.

The Vanguard Total World Stock exchange-traded fund covers more than 98% of the global investable market capitalization by holding approximately 8,000 common stocks in 47 countries. This exceptionally-broad index fund has an exceptionally-low annual expense ratio of just 0.11%.[10.25]

Exchange-traded funds like this can be held in brokerage accounts that offer checking and that offer debit cards. Brokerage-account holders invest their funds themselves and earn higher returns, so these checking and debit fees reflect the actual costs for providing these services. Banking-account holders leave the investing in the hands of the banks, and the banks earn most of the returns; these checking and debit fees reflect subsidized costs, so they're lower. Brokerage accounts, given their investment returns to the account holders, offer greater returns on net after fees are deducted.

There would be a few mostly-optional missing links:

- Brokerages would need to enable users to have their checks and debit transactions drawn on exchange-traded funds.
- Brokerages could grow and innovate to complete small-size, very-high-volume purchases and sales very efficiently.
- Stock exchanges could grow and innovate to complete small-size, very-high-volume purchases and sales very efficiently.

10.24

Fractional-Reserve Banking

- Funds could grow and innovate to complete asset purchases and sales very efficiently.

- Funds could be harmonized or standardized, or at least could recognize each other's funds as assets very efficiently. The obvious accurate way to do this is to calculate the exchange value of a fund by calculating the net asset value of the fund's current holdings at the instant the fund is used in a check or debit transaction.

- Users would need to understand well enough that no other possible money comes remotely close to matching common stocks' increases in real value over the long term.

Any or all of these moving parts could outgrow the bounds of their origins and work together to provide common-stock money.

Or, money companies could assemble all the required operations internally from the ground up.

A money company could offer a money unit that corresponds to a fractional share of ownership of a large pool of common stock; for example— and probably most ideally—this pool could be all publicly-traded common stock worldwide. Say that a $1/10^{15}$ share of this pool (a very-small fraction that in the metric system goes by the prefix "femto-", from the Danish word for 15, femten)[10.26] is a new kind of money unit called a femtoshare, which currently would be worth about 7 cents.[10.27]

When a customer used some existing money like dollars to create a deposit in femtoshares, this would amount to buying whatever fraction of the world's common stock that the existing money would buy at the instantaneous exchange rate. When a customer later used some of his femtoshares to buy a product that's priced in an existing money, this would amount to selling the fraction of the world's common stock that equaled the product's sales price at the instantaneous exchange rate.

The proportions of the world's common stocks that make up a femtoshare would remain constant until new common stocks were issued; then a money company would adjust the relative amounts of its femtoshare fund's common stock holdings. When the total of its customers' femtoshare fund balances rose or fell, the money company would adjust its femtoshare fund's total common-stock holdings.

In the money company, the femtoshare fund's core operating tasks, then, would be to buy and sell common-stock shares, and to process deposit

Fractional-Reserve Banking

and withdrawal transactions. The fewer middlemen and the greater the processing efficiency, the better. The femtoshare fund's enduring value proposition would be providing customers access to a new kind of money that greatly appreciates in value. The femtoshare fund's basic function would be storing money.

Functionally, then, the femtoshares fund would be a bank. Not a bank that depends on collusion with government and special grants of privileges like the banks we have now, but a bank that's run as a business that generates good profit by adding value.[10.28] The kind of bank we've always needed, which provides household customers and business customers the best-possible help with conducting their financial operations profitably.

In whatever way that productive money is made available, each customer who chooses to use it will find that the sting of lossy money's depreciation is wiped out from that point forward. From that point forward the customer will only use the lossy money instantaneously when it's needed for purchases or payments. At all other times, the customer's assets will be either tangible assets like real estate, or productive assets like common-stock investments or productive money—in either case, assets that are protected

10.27

against the inflation of lossy money. Governments can do what they will with their lossy money, and the customer will be protected from the lossy money stock being inflated and depreciating their holdings of money. Governments can and should at minimum protect property rights by switching to a constant money stock like gold or silver, but customers will still do better by holding productive money.

In time, everyone will migrate to using productive money. Everyone will own equity throughout their lives. All the people together will own the means of production, so, ironically, a big piece of the socialist fantasy will actually be realized by people who are free. Unlike with actual socialism, here there will be no ruling oligarchy that has total ownership of all economic, political, and legal life. All people will remain free from the government, which is the birthright of all men.

This money stock will be the most-productive money that's possible. All savings in this money will instantly be made available for the uses that add the most value.

This change will be one of the very-few systemic changes big enough to permanently ratchet up the productivity that results from working smarter, which is called total-factor productivity,[10.29]

Fractional-Reserve Banking

and by doing so, to permanently ratchet up prosperity, health, and environmental quality throughout the world.[10.30]

Money can be made of lossy money stock, constant money stock, or productive money stock.

Lossy money stock violates property rights, so it's not even legal. In the same way that the Declaration of Independence was aspirational regarding freedom from slavery, the Constitution is aspirational regarding protection of property rights. We just haven't yet had a generation of representatives implement this promise from the Constitution.

Practically-constant money stock better-secures property rights. A specific implementation of this type of money using gold or silver with 100% reserves is the only money that the Constitution authorizes the national government to coin and to regulate in value.

Productive money stock fully-secures property rights. It will more-fully deliver on this aspiration in the Constitution.

Even a dollar that's worth its weight in inert gold will pale in comparison to a femtoshare that legally equals ownership of a cross-section of the world's productive real assets.

Securing property rights is hugely valuable. Letting money develop that makes property grow in value is even better.

We don't get many chances to redesign factories using electric motors, to develop automatic industrial controls, to build out the ground transportation network, to develop the modern chemical industry.[10.29] Developing productive money will be one such step-change up, for the better.

rConstitution Paper 11
Laws Authorizing Military Action Are Unconstitutional

CONGRESSMEN IN PRIOR PARTIES *have failed to declare war and have passed, and have left in place, so-called laws authorizing violent actions that plainly are war, in defiance of the Constitution.*

Presidents in prior parties, without declarations of war, have executed, and have continued to execute, nonemergency violent actions that are plainly war, in defiance of the Constitution.[11.1]

Resistance and Strength

To secure individuals' rights from war, a nation needs both resistance and strength. Resistance prevents defeat and limits losses. Strength provides victory.[11.2]

Resistance requires military capability that can be made available rapidly.

When military capability is known to potential enemies because of open government processes or because of covert enemy processes, this military capability gets largely offset in advance by enemies who are preparing to attack. This military capability doesn't provide a comparative advantage in resistance, and both sides end up poorer.

When military capability is unknown to potential enemies, this does provide a comparative advantage in resistance. Even so, building out this military capability comes at a high cost, since building resistance depletes economic strength.

Strength requires economic superiority.

Economic superiority comes from freedom. A nation with more freedom grows more quickly than a nation with more coercion.[11.3, 11.4]

Economic superiority is decreased by military spending. Military services and goods provide destruction, not utility to satisfy needs and wants. Military spending uses up scarce resources and makes the remaining resources scarcer.[11.5]

Military spending is a kind of insurance, but counterintuitive. Military spending that's small and

Laws Authorizing Military Action

covert provides resistance, but military spending that's large depletes strength.

Military spending is also a kind of insurance that's greatly misunderstood. It's insurance against consequences that, in history, have been severe, but whose likelihoods and likely extents are now comparatively small, and can be made smaller by nations that seek peace. There is now an historically-low risk of loss due to attack by an enemy.

Since there now is relatively-less likelihood of loss from being attacked, there now is relatively-more likelihood of loss from failing to rapidly outpace the growth of murderous enemy regimes.[11.6] Empires that are grown through warmaking are inherently coercive. People working for slavemasters don't work as productively, so coercive empires are self-limited and self-destructing. Given that throughout history coercive empires have always been self-limited and have always self-destructed, people who would still choose warmaking nowadays show great ignorance. For more-free nations, an empirically-sound strategy for dealing with coercive empires or coercive nations is to wait them out.

Peace done right—with wise covert military spending and with minimal overt military spending—optimally increases a more-free nation's relative economic strength. A more-coercive nation's government thugs will see starting a war as becoming more and more certain to result in them losing everything and likely dying. If a more-free nation's government people do peace right, the nation's people can count on war becoming ever less and less likely over time.

When a more-free nation's government people stop the nation's people from growing economically strong at their potential rapid rate, this is peace done wrong.

Inadequate Resistance, and Government Destruction of Economic Strength

More-free nations' government people have a track record of doing peace wrong, but their nations have a track record of still offering resistance and having much latent strength. This can be seen for World War II by reading Table 11.1 with the war's history in mind.

At the war's start in 1939, the European Axis nations' people were outproduced by the European Allies' people by only 1.5 to 1. By organizing in advance to produce for war, designing and building advanced weapons, and organizing and heavily training people, the European Axis

Laws Authorizing Military Action

Table 11.1. World War II GDP ratios and correlates[11.7]

Year	GDP Ratio			Correlate
	Allies / Axis	European Allies / European Axis	USSR / Germany	
1938	2.4	1.6	1.0	
1939	2.3	**1.5**	1.0	**Smaller allies attacked**
1940	2.3	1.5	1.1	
1941	**2.0**	**1.0**	**0.9**	**USSR, USA attacked**
1942	2.1	1.0	0.8	
1943	2.5	1.2	1.1	
1944	3.3	1.7	1.1	
1945	**5.1**	**2.9**	1.3	**Allies won**

(Data source: Cambridge University Press)

nations' government people might have reasonably expected to rapidly defeat the European Allies. Sustaining an empire would be another matter.

Compared to production by the more-free prewar French people in 1939, production by the more coerced German-occupied French people in 1944 was less than half. Similar contractions should have been expected in other nations if they had been defeated and occupied.

The more-free UK's people and the more-coerced USSR's people unexpectedly put up enough resistance and unexpectedly grew in strength. The UK's people grew in strength because they were more free; the USSR's people grew in strength because already in peacetime the USSR had a centrally-controlled command economy like all

11.5

nations would turn to in this total war, so the USSR was able to ramp up its command economy more quickly.[11.2]

The more-free USA did not stand by idly. We survived a Pacific-island attack with plenty of resistance. Adding in the USA people's production, the Axis nations' people were outproduced by the Allies' people by a ratio that was always as large as 1941's 2.0 to 1, and that grew massively to 1945's 5.1 to 1, which proved to be overwhelming strength.

Future possible warmakers should be sobered by the Axis government people's shortsightedness and total defeat. Future peacemakers, though, who are in a position to take corrective action, should also be sobered by the Allied government people's peace done wrong.

The Allies' government people failed to use wise covert military spending to protect all their nations' people by providing adequate resistance. Also, the Allies' government people stopped their nations' people from outproducing the Axis nations' people at their long-term trend ratio of at least 3 to 1, so the Allies' government people stopped their nations' people from preventing war through economic strength.

Laws Authorizing Military Action

Of singular significance was the well-below-trend production of the USA's people due to the failures of the USA's government people.[11.8] The USA's government first grew large enough to set off the stock market crash of 1929,[11.9, v0, 11.11] and afterward grew larger and more coercive and was able to unwittingly lengthen this economic downturn into the Great Depression.[11.9, 11.12–11.14] The Great Depression in the USA, the nation with the world's largest economy, finalized the conditions under which control was achieved in Germany by the coercive National Socialist German Workers' Party—the warmaking Nazi party. The further disaster of total war finally arrived years later. It was only then that inside the USA government, the more-coercive anti-business people finally fell out of favor. The once again more-free people in business soon returned to producing up to their potential, and production snapped right back up onto its long-term trend line—back to where, absent the proliferation of more-coercive Progressive government people in the USA, production would have remained throughout the prewar years, which would have limited or prevented war by keeping up the Allies' strength.[11.15]

11.7

Changing the Things That Are within Your Control[11.16]

By attending to their own nations' resistance and economic strength—by getting their own houses in order—peacemaking ally government people stand to gain far more influence over warmaking enemy government people than by any other means, including by peace treaties, military mutual-protection treaties, and military posturing.

Resistance, as mentioned above, requires military spending that's small and covert. Economic strength requires good boundaries. To see clearly where to draw the line on whether to act or to not act, you need to clearly visualize the problems with war and with its aftermath, and you need to clearly visualize the possible alternatives.

War is destructive. A wartime economy is centrally controlled, directing scarce resources towards producing relatively-few products that are used strictly to destroy and have no peacetime benefits, and stopping scarce resources from being used to produce the many products that people need and want when people aren't threatened with death or enslavement.

Because war is destructive, war weakens the combatant nations relative to noncombatant nations.

Laws Authorizing Military Action

The increased relative weakness of the losers is physically visible. The increased relative weakness of the winners is hidden in lives lost, chronic traumas, debts piled up, and development forgone.

The combatant nations' postwar relative weakness increases the risks they face postwar from noncombatant nations, as well as from allies of convenience like the USSR in World War II.

The depleting effects of war on a nation's reserves of resistance and strength to secure individual rights postwar make it generally unwise to go to war when other potential enemy nations do not go to war.

When a more-coercive warmaking government's people threaten both a more-free peacemaking nation's people and the warmaking government's own people with death in war, reacting with comparable force is rarely the best option. One leading option, when done right, demonstrates strong confidence, strength of character, and overall strength. This option is to not respond with force immediately, and possibly to not respond with force ever.

If a more-free nation's government people never respond, the nation's people get to build economic strength.

Meanwhile, the more-coercive nation's government people who expand their territory elsewhere in the world do not build their strength like they expect. Instead, they destroy human potential on a larger scale. Plus, they spread their control more thinly over less-receptive populations.

Coercive empires fail. We may not have understood this before World War II, but we now can learn from such recent natural experiments as Germany under the National Socialist German Workers' Party; the Union of Soviet Socialist Republics; the Democratic People's Republic of Korea; the Socialist Republic of Vietnam; Cambodia under the Communist Party of Kampuchea.

If a more-free nation's government people have good boundaries, they plan covertly for adequate resistance, and whenever possible they bide their time while their people increase the nation's relative economic strength. Build a large enough advantage in relative economic strength, and would-be warmakers may not try at all, since they will surely fail.

Also, if a more-free nation's government people have good boundaries, they never telegraph their actions. That would give an enemy nation's government people cover, and the enemy nation's government people would live to fight stronger when they fight later.

Moral War

War secures the right to life most effectively when it is declared infrequently, and when it then is pursued all in.

It's a credible deterrent when an enemy nation's government people know from the past behavior of a more-free nation's government people that if the enemy nation's government people attack, their government surely will sooner or later either be destroyed by its own people or be destroyed by the more-free nation. And not only is certain destruction of the offending government a credible deterrent, it's also the only moral approach to killing in war.

When an enemy nation's government people attack a more-free nation and the more-free nation's government people do consider various responses that involve killing, the only moral response that involves killing is either to declare war and destroy the offending government and all supplier governments, or to initiate violent action and destroy the offending government and all supplier governments. The reason that war is only moral to the extent that it's directed at destroying the offending governments is because the offending governments' people are the people who are responsible for threatening both the more-free nation's people and the offending nations' people. In order for the killing that results to be a morally-justified response, the killing must be directed towards destroying the governments that are responsible for the killing. Also, in order for the killing to be a morally-justified preventive measure, the killing must be directed towards preventing the governments that are responsible from causing additional killing in future wars; and this can only be assured by destroying the governments that are responsible for the killing in the present war.

 Moral war, by necessity, is limited to using whatever military technology is available in the theatre at the time it's needed.

 Moral war is conducted with deliberate care to first and foremost keep the more-free nation's people safe, especially the more-free nation's military people, who are at obvious great risk.

 Moral war targets the enemy governments' decisionmakers, using as much force as the more-free nation's decisionmakers in their unilateral judgment think is necessary against collateral enemy combatants and enemy civilians. The resulting collateral damage varies. It depends on the enemy government people's choices to endanger the enemy nations' civilians, the more-free nation's

Laws Authorizing Military Action

military technology, the more-free nation's military preparedness, and chance. But the resulting collateral damage is always ultimately the responsibility of the enemy government people.

It is morally reprehensible to limit attacks against an enemy to protect the enemy's civilians, thinking that this is acting morally, when in fact the last century alone offers abundant evidence demonstrating that when more-coercive government people are left in place, more-coercive government people kill far more of their own civilians than are killed incidentally in wars.

In the Union of Soviet Socialist Republics, for example, world wars most-probably killed 22 million, but political suppressions most-probably killed 62 million.[11.17, 11.18] Compared to the killing in war, the killing in peace was vastly more, by a factor of 3.

More-coercive nations' governments again and again kill their nations' people in peacetime at rates that greatly exceed rates of killing in war.[11.19] This means that when a more-free nation's government people choose to not kill enemy civilians, and this decision causes the more-free nation's government people to leave in place enemy government people, this decision to not kill enemy civilians in wartime is morally wrong.

11.13

War secures the right to life most effectively for all people—in more-free nations and in more-coercive nations alike—when war is declared infrequently, and when war then is pursued all in, by the more-free nations' government people.

Peacemaking Boundaries in the Constitution

The powers not delegated to the United States by the Constitution, nor prohibited by it to the States, are reserved to the States respectively, or to the people.[11.20]

All legislative Powers herein granted shall be vested in a Congress of the United States, which shall consist of a Senate and House of Representatives.[11.21]

The Congress shall have Power …

To lay and collect Taxes, Duties, Imposts and Excises, to… provide for the common Defence … of the United States;[11.22]

To borrow Money on the credit of the United States …[11.23]

From the people, through their state representatives' ratification of the Constitution, Congress people are delegated sole power to fund war.

The Congress shall have Power …[11.22]
To provide and maintain a Navy;[11.24]

Laws Authorizing Military Action

To exercise exclusive Legislation in all Cases whatsoever... over all Places purchased by the Consent of the Legislature of the State in which the Same shall be, for the Erection of Forts, Magazines, Arsenals, dock-Yards, and other needful Buildings;[11.25]

To raise and support Armies, but no Appropriation of Money to that Use shall be for a longer Term than two Years;[11.26]

To provide for calling forth the Militia to execute the Laws of the Union, suppress Insurrections and repel Invasions;[11.27]

To provide for organizing, arming, and disciplining, the Militia, and for governing such Part of them as may be employed in the Service of the United States, reserving to the States respectively, the Appointment of the Officers, and the Authority of training the Militia according to the discipline prescribed by Congress ...[11.28]

Given power to fund war, Congress people are delegated sole power to provide a navy, provide defenses, raise armies, and provide for the militia.

The Congress shall have Power ...[11.22]

To define and punish ... Offences against the Law of Nations;[11.29]

To ... make Rules concerning Captures on Land and Water;[11.30]

11.15

> *To make Rules for the Government and Regulation of the land and naval Forces …*[11.31]

Given power to provide armed forces, Congress people are delegated sole power to define rules of engagement.

A starting point in designing ROEs right is to understand ROEs as being decision-support tools that, as a life-or-death matter for their users, need to be suitable for their intended purpose. ROEs are used in hazardous conditions. ROE users are decisionmakers on the front lines on battlefields, who decisionmakers in politics have placed at serious imminent risk of death, physical injury, and trauma, including trauma arising specifically from their decisions supported by these ROEs[11.32]—decisions that need to be made rapidly, and that once made, can't be unmade.

Battlefield decisions are cognitively challenging. ROEs need to be tools for rapidly making decisions that protect our people's safety and that are fully supported by our laws and by our government people.

ROEs constructed of pages of text are cognitively disabling, and therefore dangerous to users. It's morally wrong to give such disabling ROEs to people facing combat.

Laws Authorizing Military Action

ROE cards, though, can be good decision-support tools, if they can be appropriately simplified for rapid reference. This can be done best by focusing from the start on moral war. Moral war provides maximum safety to our people in combat. As described earlier, moral war focuses on destroying enemy governments.

Focusing on destroying enemy governments immediately changes the arc of engagements. Any means that bypass the main defenses and directly take the fight to the enemy governments are pursued vigorously. Nonessential, inconclusive attacks—which can be anything from attacks on massed conventional forces to attacks on guerillas in cities—are avoided and minimized.

ROE cards with straightforward decision criteria can help increase safety further by enabling military after-action reviews[11.33] to produce additional learning from near misses: events that could have resulted in harm to military people or materiel. Ongoing near misses increase the chances of future harm,[11.34] so learning to reduce future near misses can greatly reduce future harm.[11.35]

Our world's most lawyer-heavy military[11.36] creates adversarial relationships that make people more likely to reveal selected details that put the people in the best light, and to not tell the full stories. The opposite is what's needed for safety. People take actions that seem right to them at the time, and these same circumstances could happen to other people in the future. People's stories explaining their thinking and explaining their actions provide a powerful mechanism to enable other people to learn from mistakes without repeating the mistakes; to walk through the problem, recognize the pitfalls, and come up with new approaches and different actions to take in the future that will be safer. People's full stories can contribute powerfully to creating more safety in the future.[11.37]

Our people need to know, in particular, that it's a serious, life-threatening error to train our people to kill enemies and then to require our people to not kill enemies until enemies are about to fire on them first. If our people repeatedly spin that roulette wheel, that guarantees that more of our people will be killed. Our people need to not be wrongfully put in harm's way.

Our people need to have full support in this from all of their leadership, starting, constitutionally, with our Congress people insisting on moral terms of engagement, formulating aligned

Laws Authorizing Military Action

decision-support ROE cards, and knowing that the buck stops there.[11.38]

Moral war can most-greatly improve safety of our people in combat without degrading safety of civilians if our Congress people learn from the enemy military combatants' deceptions and change the rules so that such deceptions will no longer work against us. This can be done with minimum loss of the element of surprise by, in advance, blanketing entire enemy nations with clear warnings of new, proactive rules of engagement.[11.39] These rules should be simple and explicit, as shown in Table 11.2.

Table 11.2. Rules of Engagement (ROE) card given theatre-wide warning

Enemy involvement	Action advised
Weapon carried	Kill
Intelligence provided	Kill
Housing provided	Kill/Destroy
Transportation provided	Kill/Destroy
Supplies provided	Kill/Destroy
Captured	Detain (1-2 yr review)
Uninvolved civilian	Try to limit harm, but attack enemy

Under this ROE card, the enemy would be attacked much more precisely if we were more precise at identifying people who carry weapons, people who provide intelligence to the enemy, and housing, transportation, and supplies that are provided to the enemy. Maybe it will be possible to do this identification more precisely in moral wars through increased use of artificial intelligence, area surveillance, and nonlethal weapons that are developed anyway for civilian use. In general, though, these developments and deployments would cost considerable money. That means that developing and deploying such technology for moral-war use would generally be destructive and would reduce our relative economic strength. Such spending would therefore be counterproductive.

Rather than weakening ourselves creating more-palatable warfighting, what's far preferable is limiting such spending, increasing more rapidly in strength, and as a result removing from warmaking any profit, and therefore any incentive. Even using past technology, and certainly using current technology, it's quite feasible for a more-free peacemaking government's people to change their own behavior, both during peace and during war. And such feasible, unilateral changes are the best way to lead a more-coercive warmaking government's people to change their own behavior so they don't start wars.

Laws Authorizing Military Action

The Congress shall have Power ...[11.22] *To declare War, grant Letters of Marque and Reprisal ...*[11.30] *No person shall be ... deprived of life, liberty, or property, without due process of law ...*[11.40]

Given power to define rules of engagement, Congress people are delegated sole power to declare war and to initiate violent action. Declaring war puts all people of one nation at war against all people of another nation. Granting letters of marque and reprisal (authorizing grantees to cross borders and seize property and prisoners to redress injuries by foreign governments or subjects) puts some people of one nation into limited violent action against all people of another nation.[11.41] So Congress people have sole power to place all people into violent action, and Congress people have sole power to place some people into violent action.

Apart from when Congress people declare war or grant letters of marque and reprisal, Congress people are required to not deprive any person of life.

This means that Congress people have the sole means and opportunity to fund men and material for war or limited violence, to regulate specifically what conduct is allowable when engaging in war or limited violence, to declare war or limited violence, and to continue war or limited violence to its only moral conclusion.

11.21

The representatives who are answerable for committing us to a war are also the representatives who are answerable for using our men and resources effectively throughout the war. The rules of engagement and the declaration of war that can harm a citizen are not the responsibility of the unelected military operational people and lawyers. The rules of engagement and the declaration of war that can harm a citizen are not the responsibility of the elected president. The rules of engagement and the declaration of war that can harm a citizen are solely the responsibility of the elected Congress people.

The Congress people should be universally understood as bearing the supervisory responsibility for war and for violent action, from the highest level of the strategic declaration to the lowest level of the tactical rules. The elected Congress people should be the people who everyone expects to visit the families of our people who are killed in a war and to visit our people who are injured in a war. This is simply right. Hiding behind military people and lawyers and presidents is simply wrong.

Security from war requires resistance and strength. Resistance to attack by enemies requires

Laws Authorizing Military Action

covertly spending just enough to prevent initial defeat and to limit initial losses; strength to defeat enemies requires maximizing economic freedom.

Failures by our government people—in fighting past wars, in slowing our nation's people from growing economically stronger, in preparing suboptimally for future wars—incentivize enemy government people to attack.

When war is declared, we suddenly jump out of the normal moral equilibrium and land in a new moral equilibrium, with a new moral imperative: all enemy governments must be destroyed. All decisionmakers who threaten our people and their own people must be stopped forever. If leaders are killed and some fighters still threaten our people and their people, these fighters also must be stopped forever.

Comprehensive, detailed supervisory control of war prevention, rules of engagement, initiation, and support is solely delegated to Congress people. Providing smart resistance, protecting freedom that increases economic strength, providing resources and rules that protect our military people and give us decisive military advantages, choosing to fight morally by destroying enemy governments—all this decisive control is not in the hands of unelected military people, or presidents. This is Congress people's job.

We need to be able to choose Congress people who will do their job.

rConstitution Paper 12
Block Grants Are Unconstitutional

CONGRESSMEN IN PRIOR PARTIES *have passed, and have left in place, so-called laws creating block grants that use monetary incentives to control state actions, in defiance of the Constitution. Presidents in prior parties have signed and executed, and have continued to execute, so-called laws creating block grants that use monetary incentives to control state actions, in defiance of the Constitution.*[12.1]

Block Grants Are Big Government

National-government spending on state governments is of three types, listed in order of increasing national-government control: general revenue sharing, block grants, and categorical grants.[12.2]

General-revenue sharing since 1986 has been zero.[12.3] Block-grant spending is comparatively small. Categorical-grant spending dominates by a ratio of 11 to 1.[12.4, 12.5]

Block grants are the spending currently in use that offers the least control by the national government, so they are worth examining. The conclusions that apply to block grants, with which the national government applies the least control, will apply even more strongly to categorical grants, with which the national government applies more control.

In practice, the "block grant" label basically functions as marketing copy that gets voters more willing to accept this spending at the outset. The label is transient. Once spending starts, the spending type always changes dynamically.

These are slush funds. They're all about politics. Just like with the tax code, any atypical simplification is always followed by incessant complexification.[12.6] Block grants get changed into categorical grants, categorical grants get changed into new subtypes. Almost every change increases the national government's control. The control

Block Grants

can be a byproduct, where the goal is just to cut these pork pies into ever-thinner slices to more-precisely favor political cronies. But regardless of what rationales lead the government people to act, this spending is always accompanied by control that's exerted by the national government on state governments.

The scope of national-government spending on states is 62% on health, with the remainder on income, transportation, education / social services, development, and other scope.[12.5] Zooming in closer, the scope is highly diverse, and includes agriculture, environmental, interior, and policing.[12.7] The pork pushers run wild.

This scope is excluded from the national government by the Constitution's strictly-enumerated powers. The national-government's enumerated scope is limited to political scope to make peace and war, commercial scope to increase commerce freedom, and support scope to operate the national government.[12.8]

Comparing the national government's enumerated scope to the national-government spending on states, the amount of this block-grant and categorical-grant spending that's constitutional is zero.

12.3

Ending that national-government spending immediately is therefore required by the supreme law. Ending that spending immediately is also the best practice.

Government Spending Is the Worst

In government, fast change is always best. When the change is for the better, fast change quickly brings results that are good, which helps the change go farther and endure. When the change is temporarily for the worse, fast change quickly brings results that are bad, which helps the bad change get reversed fully and get replaced quickly with change for the better.[12.1]

In the case of national-government spending on states, the national-government people can and should immediately end their spending and immediately reduce national taxes accordingly. The state-government people can immediately increase their spending and immediately increase their taxes, but they can and should do both the spending and the taxing in ways that more-faithfully represent the policy desires of each state's people.

Returning scope from the national-government people back to the state-government

Block Grants

people enables the scope to be provided more efficiently, with more built-in competition that automatically improves efficiency. Going further by returning scope from the state-government people back to customers enables the scope to be provided the most efficiently, with the most built-in competition that automatically improves efficiency.

These returns of scope will get us back to doing what worked well for us back when we were poorer. This will work well for us again because this will increase competition and efficiency by breaking the strangleholds of the national-government people's national monopoly and of the state-government people's state monopolies. Every bit of scope that's freed from the government monopolists' control, which is slow and unresponsive, is immediately subjected to customers' control, which is fast and unrelenting.

The differences between control by government monopolists and control by customers are hard to see in words from economists and politicians and media people. But these differences in control are easy to see in graphics from an engineer, Figure 12.1.

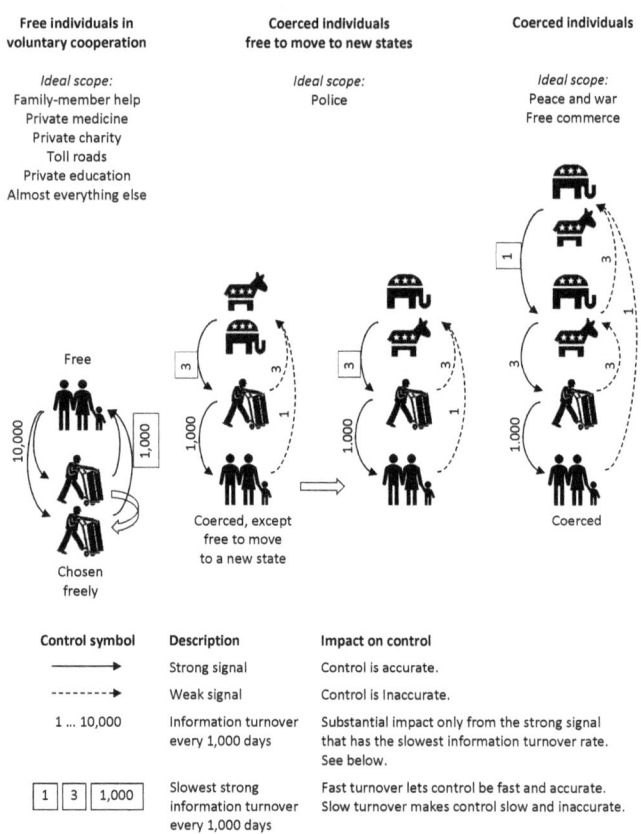

Figure 12.1. Free customers drive efficiency and innovation.

Free Cooperation Is Best

The leftmost column shows the control interactions when free customers and producers voluntarily cooperate. The symbol for a family is located on the top to reflect that customers are in control. The symbol for a worker moving a product is located at the bottom to reflect that producers are controlled by customers' choices.

Producers choose tentative production rates, pay people to discover and mine raw materials, pay people to design products, choose asking prices, pay people to build plants and equipment, and pay people to manufacture products. Producers can't know upfront what will be the actual production rates and the actual sale prices. These actual numbers determine how much value the producers have added.

Customers consider all they know about their own needs and wants and about all services and goods available now and in the future. They look for the best values that match producers' services and goods to their own needs and wants, and they decide to buy or to not buy from individual producers. These free choices are indicated in the graphic by depicting two individual producers who the customer family freely chooses between.

Customers' choices, taken together, control producers' actual production rates and actual sale prices, which finalizes producers' actual value added. When customers don't choose a producer, this finalizes that the producer must improve or go out of business. These final numbers firm up very quickly.

Customers decide on purchases within, say, two hours. This means that their purchasing decision introduces a delay into the system that has a delay time of roughly 1/10 of a day. Producers ship products to customers within a delay time of roughly 1 day. When delay times are all relatively small—like here, where free people voluntarily cooperate—control can be very good.[12.9]

In the figure, the numbers listed aren't delay times but instead are the corresponding information-turnover rates. An information-turnover rate is the reciprocal of the corresponding delay time. The reciprocal of a quantity is the number 1 divided by the quantity. For example, in the case of customers' purchasing decisions:

$$\begin{aligned} Information-turnover\ rate &= \frac{1}{delay\ time} \\ &= \frac{1}{\frac{1}{10}\ day} \\ &= 10\ \frac{1}{day} \\ &= 10\ times\ a\ day \end{aligned}$$

With delay times, a smaller number is better for control, while with information-turnover rates,

Block Grants

a larger number is better for control. Information-turnover rates are shown in the figure so that a larger number indicates that control can be better. But there's a further consideration. Where the information-turnover rates are larger, the information turnover is faster; and where the information turnover is faster, this information turnover barely limits the quality of the control in the system. What most-greatly limits the quality of the control in the system is whichever information-turnover rate in the system is the smallest.

So then when the smallest information-turnover rate in a system is large, control throughout the system can be fast and accurate.

When the information signals are also strong throughout the loop—both in the forward direction and in the return direction (the "feedback" direction)—control can be more accurate.

When free individuals voluntarily cooperate, all the information-turnover rates are large, dramatically larger than when state-government people or national-government people exercise monopoly control. This means that when free individuals voluntarily cooperate, the control can be and is much, much better. Customers relentlessly search out the best values, decide quickly, and relentlessly shun lower-value products. To survive,

12.9

producers must stay competitive at adding value. As the figure's caption summarizes, customers relentlessly drive producers to add value more efficiently by innovating.

Coercion by State-Government People

The figure's center two columns show the control interactions when state-government people grab control.

The icons used to represent government people show that government people's decisions are driven by the people in the two major parties, the Democrats and the Republicans.

In these center columns there's just one layer of government, the governments of the states. Now it's the state-government people who control the producers. State-government people are taken to be making purchasing decisions on roughly one year's worth of products at a time. That means that the information-turnover rates between state-government people and producers are dramatically smaller: just once a year. Also, the feedback from producers is weaker, since state-government people don't have to listen; being monopolists, they can dictate their own terms, take it or leave it. The control in this supervisory-control loop is bad.

Block Grants

Producers are depicted here as delivering just as fast as when they're in voluntary cooperation. But here, producers just drop their products on families, and the producers aren't affected at all by direct feedback from families. Families send their feedback to state-government people, by voting just once every 2 years or 4 years. In this situation where information-turnover rates are even smaller—just 1/2 per year or 1/4 per year—control is even worse.[12.9]

Slow information turnover makes it impossible to see what change is underway elsewhere in the system, so it's impossible to start making corrections that will help. Control is harmed the most by the information-turnover rate that's the smallest. Control is harmed a little more by the other information-turnover rates that are larger.[12.10]

In such systems with control by government people, the feedback is not only very slow but also very weak. Each individual vote is just for a single candidate who is a limited selection from the duopoly of the two major parties. Plus, each candidate is, in effect, a bundle of some policies that voters support, together with some policies that voters don't support, and voters only get the choice to take it or leave it.

For government-controlled products, customers now have their money taken from them by force by the government people. Customers who were in voluntary cooperation would be in control at the top of the food chain, but customers for government-controlled products are pushed to the bottom of the food chain, eating table scraps, subservient.

Still, when products are controlled by state-government people, one choice remains available to customers: customers are free to move to a new state. This choice is highlighted by using two columns to represent two different states. Making this choice would be costly, so most customers don't make this choice unless they're forced to move to get a job. Even so, it's this remaining choice to move, more than the choices made in voting between candidates from our current Progressive major parties, that can significantly influence the state-government people. The reason is that this choice significantly changes states' populations at the margin, as customers who are younger relocate relatively quickly to states that offer better employment prospects, because these states offer more freedom.

Coercion by National-Government People Too

The figure's rightmost column shows that this single remaining option is taken away when national-government people grab control.

Here, there are two layers of government: the nation's government and the states' governments. The national-government people control the state-government people, and the state-government people control the producers. Now there are two control loops in series, and in each of these control loops the control is bad.

The national-government people are taken to be making significantly-different purchasing decisions not once every year, but instead just once every 2 years or 4 years—every congressional election or every presidential election. Once the national-government people finally adjust their control decisions, the state-government people are given credit for adjusting their control decisions the year after that.

The customers are two levels removed from control. At the highest level of supervisory control, the national-government people are the masters controlling the state-government people who are the slaves.[12.11] At the next-highest level of supervisory control, the state-government people are the masters controlling the producers who are the slaves.

Now in both supervisory loops the control is bad. Also, now in the bottom-level slave loop where the producers finally deliver to customers, the customers can no longer influence their masters by relocating in a new state, because the national-government monopoly is in place in all states.

The abysmal control of the whole tottering system headed by national-government people is a recipe for inefficiency and stagnation,[12.12] as is clear from a quick look at the unwieldy stackup of controllers with its information-turnover rates that are dramatically slower—not one, not two, but three orders of magnitude slower.

In Governments, Least Is Best

Given the progressively-worse consequences of increasingly-centralized control, the figure lists as ideal scopes:

- Maximum freedom for customers to directly control the provision of goods and services in voluntary cooperation with producers.
- Minimal state-government scope.

- Minimal national-government scope, as enumerated in the Constitution.

These ideal scopes are more than just theoretical; they're proven in practice. Voluntary cooperation has been used to supply every currently government-monopolized service and good, including military defense, medical care, help for the needy, retirement income, roads, bridges, education, social services, and disaster relief.[12.13]

As producers grow larger, they gain economies of scale,[12.14, 12.15] but they also add managers. Managers help operations work at larger scale. But managers reduce the proportion of the workforce that directly produces products, which reduces efficiency. Also, managers change the information that people at the top and people at the bottom use to make decisions, which reduces innovation and efficiency.[12.16, 12.17] The optimum number of layers of managers plus workers may be just 5.[12.18]

When a producer is organized or operated worse than others, customers vote with their feet quickly. When state-government people get in the way of customers and producers, customers vote with their feet slowly. When national-government people get in the way of customers and producers, customers are out of control and out of options.

Our major political parties leave us coerced, despite the fact that at the national level we lawfully are free, and despite the fact that at the state level we ideally would be free.

We need a new party to offer majority slates of candidates who will represent us lawfully and will leave us in maximum control of satisfying our own needs and wants.[12.1]

rConstitution Paper 13

Filibuster/Cloture Is Unconstitutional

SENATORS IN PRIOR PARTIES *have failed to pass bills by simple majorities, in defiance of the Constitution.*[13.1]

Simple-Majority Voting Is Plainly Required
What's constitutional is set out in plain language in the Constitution.

> ... *each Senator shall have one Vote.*[13.2, 13.3]

At the start of a new Senate, the senators who form the current majority immediately fail to change the standing filibuster/cloture rules, and by doing so immediately abdicate substantial constitutional power.

13.1

By not acting, the senators who have a simple majority agree to stop a normal bill from going forward if the bill is disapproved by a minority greater than 40%. From then on whenever a bill is disapproved by a minority greater than 40%, the senators who have a simple majority stop the bill from going forward.

The minority has no power to make such an agreement. The minority just represents its voters. Each minority vote counts as 1 vote.

The senators who have a simple majority have all power to make such an agreement. These senators act as if the votes in a minority of 40% have the same weight as the votes in a majority of 60%. Since each minority vote counts as 1 vote, this means that the senators who have a simple majority act as if each majority vote counts as only 2/3 of a vote.

The Constitution specifies that every vote counts as 1 vote. Each time the senators who have a simple majority stop a normal bill from going forward if the bill is disapproved by a minority greater than 40%, these senators value the minority votes fully but value their own votes at a substantial discount. These senators violate the Constitution blatantly.

Filibuster/Cloture

Through their immediate adoption of unconstitutional rules and their ongoing use of unconstitutional rules, the senators who have a simple majority fail to constitutionally represent their states' people.

The Vice President of the United States shall be President of the Senate, but shall have no Vote, unless they be equally divided.[13.4]

Typically, the vice president doesn't preside over the Senate. Once he's in office, the vice president immediately fails to act, and by doing so immediately abdicates substantial constitutional power.

In the vice president's absence, the senators who have a simple majority agree to stop a normal bill from going forward if the bill is disapproved by a minority greater than 40%. This means that the senators who have a simple majority stop a normal bill from going forward if the votes are equally divided.

The Constitution specifies that if the votes are equally divided, the vice president has the vote that breaks the tie. When the vice president and the senators who have a simple majority treat the vice president's vote as irrelevant, the vice

13.3

president and the senators who have a simple majority violate the Constitution blatantly.

Through his immediate and ongoing unconstitutional inaction, the vice president fails to constitutionally represent the nation's people. Through their immediate and ongoing unconstitutional actions, the senators who have a simple majority fail to constitutionally represent their states' people.

Every Bill which shall have passed the House of Representatives and the Senate, shall, before it become a Law, be presented to the President of the United States: If he approve he shall sign it, but if not he shall return it, with his Objections to that House in which it shall have originated, who shall enter the Objections at large on their Journal, and proceed to reconsider it. If after such Reconsideration two thirds of that House shall agree to pass the Bill, it shall be sent, together with the Objections, to the other House, by which it shall likewise be reconsidered, and if approved by two thirds of that House, it shall become a Law.[13.5]

The Constitution's first line of defense against government power is to separate powers and create offsetting powers. A bill is initially passed by Congress people who were elected by simple majorities. A bill is vetoed by a president who was

Filibuster/Cloture

elected by a simple majority. It only makes sense that the bill is initially passed by simple majorities. A fallback protection in the Constitution is a supermajority for enumerated votes. To override a veto, the Constitution requires supermajorities of 67%. This would make little difference if for initial passage the Constitution required a supermajority in the Senate of 60%. But this makes a substantial difference since for initial passage the Constitution requires simple majorities of 50%.

This Constitution ... shall be the supreme Law of the Land ...[13.6]
Each House may determine the Rules of its Proceedings ...[13.7]

Congressmen may not violate the state-ratified Constitution with congressionally-created rules.

Simple-Majority Voting Is Always Best

When elected representatives are required through simple-majority voting to stand up and be counted, their representation becomes valid. Representation that's valid brings change that's fast. Change that's fast is best in all cases.

When change is for the better, change that's fast makes sure that changes that are good are more complete. As shown in Figure 13.1, change that's fast has made sure that the people in some nations in the former Soviet sphere have been able to spend many more years of their lives in economic freedom that's much greater.

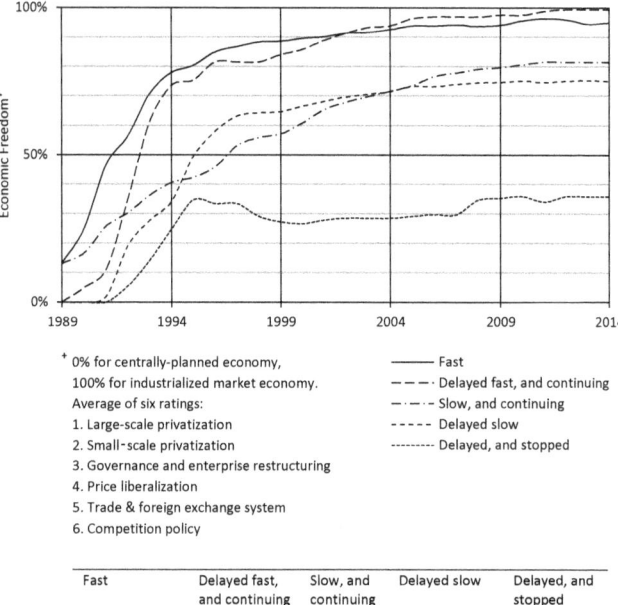

Figure 13.1. After the Berlin Wall was torn down, fast change brought good results fast, and the progress kept up. (Figure courtesy of James Anthony) [13.1, 13.8, 13.9]

When change is for the worse, change that's fast ensures that change that's bad is felt fast, so reversal to change that's good comes fast.

This healthy cleansing mechanism is well understood by the people who create legislation that's bad. These people try their best to make it so that legislation that's bad doesn't become effective all at once, but instead phases in over a time period that's very long. The goodies come first, and voters are portrayed as hooked; the costs come later, and voters are portrayed as acceptant.

Legislative phase-ins not only are against our interests, they also are unconstitutional grabs of executive power. The legislative power is the power to write laws, which are solely rules coupled with sanctions (threatened penalties). Decisions on when to execute laws are not laws. Decisions on when to execute laws are exercises of executive power, and the executive power is vested in the president.[13.10]

The many unconstitutional actions of our elected representatives clearly are self-sustaining. Ever since we've had a Constitution, we've had at least some government people who have defied the Constitution, and this way of attacking freedom became mainstream long ago.

Throughout the Progressives' century[13.11] we've had supermajorities of representatives in every Congress who have defied the Constitution, and we've had representatives nominated and elected as president almost every term who have defied the Constitution.[13.1] Simply telling our representatives we're unhappy with them, or voting them out of office, or term-limiting them out of office, won't change a thing. Our major parties will simply nominate new Progressive candidates, like they're designed to do.

We need a new party designed with structural safeguards like those of the Constitution that will keep the party grassroots sovereign, and further designed to reliably nominate candidates who, in office, follow the Constitution.

The legal authority is there. The Constitution provides all the preexisting legal structure that's needed.

The votes are there. Voters have been voting for the most-constitutional major-party candidates who are on the ballots in 2010, 2012 except for president, 2014, and 2016.

What has been missing has been a party that nominates true representatives, who follow the Constitution by fully exercising their constitutional powers to offset the powers of others in

government.¹³·¹ Nominate true representatives, and they will represent the sovereign people and states.
Including in Senate voting.

rConstitution Paper 14

Unadvised and Unconsented Treaties Are Unconstitutional

SENATORS IN PRIOR PARTIES have refused to advise and consent on treaties negotiated by presidents, and congressmen in prior parties have passed or have left in place so-called laws supporting the treaties, in defiance of the Constitution.[14.1]

Treaties Are Law

No State shall, without the Consent of Congress, ... enter into any Agreement or Compact ... with a foreign Power ...[14.2]

No State shall enter into any Treaty ...[14.3]

An agreement or compact is a pact about a matter of temporary interest that requires an act to be performed once and be done with. Changing a state boundary line, for example.

A treaty is a pact between nations for their people's welfare. Typically, a treaty will require acts that must continue for as long as the treaty exists, but a treaty can instead just require an act to be performed once and be done with.[14.4]

The Constitution doesn't delegate to national-government people the power to make agreements or compacts. This means that to constitutionally make an agreement or compact with another nation, the national-government people must make a treaty.[14.5]

This Constitution, and the Laws of the United States which shall be made in Pursuance thereof; and all Treaties made, or which shall be made, under the Authority of the United States, shall be the supreme Law of the Land ...[14.6]

Treaties are national-government law.

Laws Are Limited

The powers not delegated to the United States by the Constitution, nor prohibited by it to the States, are reserved to the States respectively, or to the people.[14.5]

The Congress shall have Power ...[14.7]

Unadvised and Unconsented Treaties

[The President] shall take Care that the Laws be faithfully executed ...[14.8]

The national government is limited.

Its powers are defined with respect to its laws: legislating laws, executing laws, and judging cases.

Its laws are limited to a few enumerated scope areas. The national government is delegated specific powers for preventing or fighting war, facilitating commerce, and operating itself.[14.9]

Since treaties are law, and national-government law is limited to specific powers in a few enumerated scope areas, constitutional treaties can only cover specific powers in those scope areas: preventing or fighting war, and facilitating commerce.

Presidents Aren't Lawmakers

The President ... shall have Power, by and with the Advice and Consent of the Senate, to make Treaties, provided two thirds of the Senators present concur ...[14.10]

National-government law is constitutionally produced either by combined action of people with legislative power and people with executive power, or by concerted action by people with legislative power. Treaties are constitutionally produced only by combined action of senators and presidents.

14.3

"By the advice of the Senate" means when advised in advance by 2/3 of senators present. "With the advice of the Senate" means using explicit advance and in-process advice from 2/3 of senators present. "By and with the consent of the Senate" means if and only if authorized afterwards by 2/3 of senators present. In treatymaking, the Senate has the power.

A president acts as the Senate's agent.[14.11]

A president has no constitutional power to pass a statute, but a president has power to execute a statute. Because a president has this power to execute a statute, it makes sense that after a bill passes and before it becomes a statute, a president has power to either sign, indicating that in his judgment the bill can constitutionally be executed and should become law, or veto, indicating that in his judgment the bill can't constitutionally be executed or shouldn't become law.

A president has no constitutional power to initiate a treaty, to make a treaty without prior and ongoing advice, or to enact a treaty without consent; but a president has power to execute a treaty. Because a president has this power to execute a treaty, it makes sense that as part of treatymaking, a president has power to either sign, indicating that in his judgment the treaty can constitutionally be executed and should become law, or veto, indicating that in his judgment the treaty can't constitutionally be executed or shouldn't become law.

Since treaties are law, it's entirely appropriate that constitutionally, the Senate controls treaties before negotiation, during negotiation, and at completion of negotiation.

Nowadays with instant communications, direct Senate control of the work in process is readily feasible and offers every advantage. To instead have surrogates work out details in advance, conduct presidential meetings that are just photo ops, and drop a treaty proposal on an uninvolved Senate—each such action would brazenly defy the Constitution.

The Constitution denies presidents the sovereign treaty power that had been exercised by kings. The Constitution vests control of treaty-making in the Senate.

Unilateral Actions Are Strong

Life's most-important moments happen mostly at home, some at work, less in international work, and least in government people working with other government people.

Work, both domestic and international, mostly consists of business people working with other business people. People benefit on both sides, so people voluntarily cooperate in ways that are ever more varied and intricate.

Government work is different. Government people benefit, but even if the rest of the people don't benefit, the rest of the people are compelled by force to participate anyway. Because of this, government people need their scopes limited. National-government people need their scopes exceptionally limited. National-government people's proper scope is just to prevent or fight war, and to facilitate commerce.[9]

In these areas, treaties have been around since back when treaties were with kings, so treaties undoubtedly are valuable, you might naturally expect. That expectation would be dead wrong.

Treaties are slow and weak.

The stronger nation's government people receive PR and give stuff away. The weaker nation's government people, who are generally coercive, get strengthened. For the people in both nations, it's lose-lose.

The root problem with treaties is that to their core, treaties are boundary violations. In treaties, a nation's government people fail to protect their

Unadvised and Unconsented Treaties

nation's own boundaries, and the nation's government people violate other nations' boundaries.

When our nation was formed, our military forces were underpowered and unproven, and our commerce was vulnerable to the actions of other established nations' government people. Treaties seemed vital, and treaties seemed to help. But those circumstances were exceptional and temporary. Once a nation is established, treaties turn clearly problematic.

In treaties, each nation's government people want something from the other nations' government people. They focus on actions of the other nations' government people, actions that they themselves really have no control over. This is how they violate boundaries. Each nation's government people try to exert control outside the boundaries of where they themselves have power, and each nation's government people try to exert control inside the boundaries of where other nations' government people have power. This focus on trying to control other people takes time, time in excess of the time it takes to perform the domestic actions that each nation's government people have control over. In the end, a treaty's government partners each just do only what they themselves want to do. Treaties waste the extra time that it takes to make treaties, and treaties deliver no added control, actions, or value.

Unilateral actions are fast and strong.

The speed comes from a nation's government people focusing on what they have control over. The number of people who have to take action is minimized, and their actions are limited to actions that the people themselves have control over. Unilateral actions are done at maximum speed.

The strength of unilateral actions comes from the nation's government people doing no harm, and doing everything they can that's helpful.

Unilateral actions avoid harm from government people giving people's stuff away. If a treaty partner is an enemy, then giving the enemy stuff harms your people by taking away their stuff and harms your people by strengthening the enemy. If a treaty partner is a friend, then giving the friend stuff harms your people by taking away their stuff. Take away the treatymaking PR smokescreen, and the naked losses that giveaways are is easier to see and harder to rationalize. Giveaways and their harms are then easier to avoid.

Unilateral actions lead government people to do all that's helpful because unilateral actions eliminate the treatymaking PR smokescreen. This makes it easier to see all the unilateral actions that

Unadvised and Unconsented Treaties

are available, and to see which of these unilateral actions are helpful.

If another nation's government people offensively threaten people with death in war or abuse people, then limiting trade between their nation's people and our nation's people weakens their government people's ability to harm us or others. Congress people should enact substantial tariffs across the board on imports from the enemy nation. Congress people also should outlaw all exports to the enemy nation that have military value that's non-negligible. Acting across the board on imports from an enemy and on military exports to an enemy avoids crony side-deals that would weaken the aggregate impact; so when taking unilateral actions on an enemy, acting across the board makes the actions maximally broad for maximum strength.

If another nation's government people defensively protect people from death in war and respect people, then maximizing their people's commerce with our nation's people strengthens them and us. Congress people should eliminate tariffs across the board on imports from the friendly nation, and legalize all exports to the friendly nation. Acting across the board on imports from a friend and on military exports to a friend once again avoids crony side deals that would weaken the aggregate impact; so when taking unilateral actions on a friend, just like when taking unilateral actions on an enemy, acting across the board makes the actions maximally broad for maximum strength.

Of course, acting unilaterally on tariffs on imports allows the other nation's government people to impose tariffs on your exports.

If they do, their tariffs do net harm to their people. A few cronies get to keep jobs temporarily. The cronies seek protection only because they are uncompetitive already, and given protection they just fall further behind. In the end they lose more jobs than they would have lost in free and open competition. All the while, all their people pay more for the products they buy. The added cost to a large number of consumers is greater than the added income to a few cronies, so the entire nation's standard of living is reduced.

Meanwhile, your government people's zero tariffs do net good for your nation's people. Potential cronies gain nothing. Lacking protection, they compete harder than ever, and as a direct result they stay competitive internationally. In the end they employ more people than they would have under crony protection-induced atrophy. All the while, all your nation's people pay less for the products they buy. The large, permanent benefits

Unadvised and Unconsented Treaties

to customers significantly outweigh the smaller, temporary costs to potential cronies, so your entire nation's standard of living is increased.

With government people who are known enemies, relations are best limited by Congress people quickly.

With government people who in the past were known enemies but who may possibly be turning friendly, relations are best warmed up by Congress people slowly, with all due diligence. First, the known enemy's government people should volunteer to be overwhelmingly open, we should examine their threat potential and all relevant behavior exhaustively, and we should be confident that they are fully worthy of trust. We should remain ready to reverse course quickly if we later find otherwise.

With regimes that are genuinely overturned and trustworthy, relations are best embraced by Congress people quickly.

In a nutshell, if the government people in another nation behave like the government people in one of our states, then Congress people should treat them like one of our states;[14.12] and if the government people in another nation prepare for war, then we should prepare for war.

Fast, complete action flipping between the two extreme stable states of unilateral maximally-open trade and unilateral maximally-restricted trade provides optimum benefits to our own people, and does this using actions that are entirely within our own control.

Such fast, complete action flipping between the two extreme stable states also provides maximum control action to influence other nations' government people. Even though other nations' government people are independent of our control, this action incentivizes them best to act in the best interests of their people and of our people.

These unilateral, maximal actions don't just leave the option of war still on the table (which in reality it always is); these unilateral, maximal actions also build our nation and our natural allies to maximum strength, and deplete our enemies down to minimum strength.

Also, these unilateral, maximal actions serve as the best-possible model for natural allies to follow. And if economic access to the world's-largest trading partner is already irreplaceable, then, surely, economic access to the world's remaining trading partners is an incentive that's nearly irresistible. An increasingly-peaceful world will continue to enforce this incentive increasingly well, and will reap the benefits.

Unadvised and Unconsented Treaties

Interestingly, and helpfully, it's built into the Constitution that unilateral action can more-easily be fast and complete. Unilateral action only requires the support of simple majorities of Congress people plus the president (or of 2/3 majorities of Congress people without the president).[14.13, 14.14] Treaties require support of 2/3 majorities of the Senate people present, plus the president.[14.10] Simple majorities of Congress people can act more quickly and completely than 2/3 majorities of the Senate people present.

Unilateral action works better and is more practical, so this should be the end of the story. But since people don't all recognize this, for the time being let's play along further to better understand how treaties should work constitutionally.

Treaties Can Be Jumpstarts

Suppose that instead of Congress people and a president taking unilateral action, Senate people want Senate people and a president to make a treaty. There are two aspects of treatymaking to consider: what terms would make a treaty good for the USA, and what terms would pass the Senate and be agreed to by a president. First, what terms would make a treaty good for the USA?

Here, the answer is simple. In a treaty that's good for the USA, the USA will take the exact same actions that are good for the USA to take as unilateral actions; no more, and no less.

Contrary to conventional wisdom, it is bad to make treaties with enemies.

The problem is that the USA follows through on its obligations in treaties, but enemies cheat. Enemies only comply with whatever treaty terms they would choose to act on unilaterally anyway without a treaty.

Enemy-government people only agree to a treaty because our government people offer to give them something we wouldn't give them otherwise. Typically, we offer them direct aid, and we offer them freer trade. Both are useful to the enemy government militarily, and both strengthen the enemy government.

Making a treaty with enemy-government people amounts to having our government people negotiate with themselves. They work themselves up determining to get to a meaningless signing ceremony and deceptive PR. In exchange, our government people weaken us and strengthen the enemy-government people.

The action needed when confronted by enemy-government people is the opposite. Our

Unadvised and Unconsented Treaties

government people need to strengthen us and weaken the enemy-government people.

Making a treaty with government people who are proven peaceful is at least not a negative, but it doesn't add value. And any time spent not adding value is time wasted.

The one time when a treaty might add value is when a nation's government people haven't yet proven peaceful, they are determined to be proven peaceful, and a treaty expedites the normally-gradual buildup of cooperation and justified trust.

When a nation's government people haven't yet proven peaceful, they present real barriers to trust that must be overcome. It is up to the nation's government people to counter past proof of untrustworthiness by volunteering present proof of trustworthiness.

They must not oppose the peaceful existence of other peaceful nations. They must not supply funding, materiel, or people to commit aggression against people of other nations. They must not commit aggression against people of their own nation.

They must not develop weapons of mass destruction. In particular, they must not process nuclear materials, develop conventional-explosive trigger designs, or develop ballistic missiles or cruise missiles. They must not possess chemical or biological weapon ingredients, and they must not develop poison-dispersion technology.

They must offer up their military R&D and military facilities for full examination by peaceful nations.

After World War II, Germany, Japan, and Italy did not keep secret military R&D and military facilities. After the Civil War, the former Confederacy did not retain military forces.

To put it simply, if a nation's government people want their people to enjoy free and open trade with our people just like the trade among our states' people, the nation's government people need to show exhaustively that they're peaceful just like our states' government people.

Treaties done right are not harmful agreements between enemies. Treaties done right are not harmfully-entangling agreements or valueless agreements between likely allies. Treaties done right are rare, helpful jumpstarts to peace and commerce for former enemy-government people who use every conceivable means to demonstrate that they're worthy of trust from now on.

Our government people's offer of free and open trade has great value. Their government people's proof of reform and openness needs to greatly engender trust.

Constitutional Senators Needed

So then, some treaties could have a positive role. It remains to be seen how likely it is that treaties done right could pass the Senate and be agreed to by a president.

Constitutionally, treatymaking would have to be initiated by the advice of 2/3 of the senators present. Treatymaking would next have to proceed with the advice of 2/3 of the senators present.

Treatymaking would have to be conducted by the president as the senators' agent.[14.11] Being the senators' agent, a president effectively can veto treaties, but a president constitutionally must execute the advice and the consent of the senators. If an agent must execute the advice and the consent of a large body of people, then relying on the agent to convey information in person risks adding much error, as always, while adding little value nowadays. Given modern communications and travel, senators and other nations' government people can now readily exchange documents, teleconference, and meet directly with one another. Presidents can monitor the progress and determine whether they would sign any resulting draft treaty.

Any resulting draft treaty would have to be consented to by 2/3 of the senators present.

We can get a better idea of whether treaty-making initiation might pass, what treaty advice might pass, and what treaty consent might pass by examining swing senators' voting records.

If a given treaty is desired more by the senators who vote in support of the Constitution relatively more often, then as of this writing the three swing votes would be Christopher Murphy, Tammy Baldwin, and Chris Van Hollen. All are Democrats, with Conservative Review Liberty Scores as low as 9%.[14,15] It's hard to visualize what provisions might get yes votes both from the senators who vote to support the Constitution relatively more often and from these swing senators who vote to support the Constitution just 1 time out of 11.

If on the other hand a given treaty is desired more by the senators who vote in defiance of the Constitution relatively more often, then as of this writing the three swing votes would be Roy Blunt, John Thune, and Richard Burr. All are Republicans, with Conservative Review Liberty Scores as high as 40%.[15] It's easier to visualize what provisions might get yes votes both from the senators who vote to defy the Constitution relatively more often and from these swing senators who vote 3 times out of 5 to defy the Constitution. It's not really reaching across the aisle when you already spend most of your time together.

Since our current representation offers no plausible path for treatymaking by people who support the Constitution, and offers a very-feasible path for treatymaking by people who defy the Constitution, in the current circumstances it's by far best that we resolutely oppose and defeat treaties.

We should bear in mind that the only constructive role of treaties is narrowly limited.

Almost always, for everyone concerned, it's best if we eschew treaties and instead act unilaterally with maximum power.

rConstitution Paper 15
NATO Is a Sham

SENATORS IN PRIOR PARTIES *have refused to advise and consent on treaties negotiated by presidents, and congressmen in prior parties have passed or have left in place so-called laws supporting the treaties, in defiance of the Constitution.*[15.1]

Moral War Must Follow the Constitution

War violates peacetime norms of moral behavior. In war, the lives of both the aggressor nation's people and the defender nation's people are threatened by the actions of the aggressor nation's government people. To be moral, war must secure the defender nation's people and must eliminate the aggressor government and its supplier governments.

Treaties can't ensure that war secures the defender nation's people. Treaties can't ensure that war eliminates the aggressor government and its supplier governments. Treaties therefore can't ensure that war is conducted morally.

The reason why treaties can't ensure that war is conducted morally is that treaties can't legally change the Constitution's scope.

The Constitution has more-restrictive ratification requirements than treaties have, so the Constitution is the more-exacting definition of what powers have been delegated by the sovereign people to the national government. The Constitution also defines the terms of treatymaking. Both the Constitution's ratification requirements and the Constitution's control of the treatymaking process logically establish that the Constitution has precedence over treaties.

Since the Constitution has precedence over treaties, and since the Constitution likewise has precedence over statutes, the Constitution solely controls what processes can legally change the Constitution's scope. These allowed processes do not include treatymaking.

This means that the Constitution totally controls the national government's scope, and treaties have no control over the national government's scope. Treaties can't legally control the scope to enable war by funding war, providing a navy, providing defenses, raising armies, providing for the militia, defining rules of engagement, declaring war, and commanding the military forces. Treaties can't legally control the scope to enable commerce.

Declaring war has immediate life-and-death consequences. Using the Constitution, this sovereign power of the people is delegated to Congress people to pass, to the president to approve or disapprove, and to Congress people to repass if necessary.

Such processes for enabling war delegate this consequential decisionmaking to representatives for each district, for each state, and for the nation, representatives who are elected by the people. Every government that's legitimate exists to secure the rights of the people, and operates by representing the people. Representing the people is the approach that's most fundamentally sound, because people's thinking is fundamentally sound in matters that require common sense.

People have the common-sense understanding that self-defense is a fundamental right. People want this right secured.

People have the common-sense understanding that war should be made as infrequent as possible. This requires resolving each war in the way that most-greatly prevents future war.

The common sense of the people in each nation can't be improved upon by treaties. The government's operation in each nation can't be improved upon by treaties. At best, either treaties redundantly call for the actions that government people would have taken even without a treaty, or treaties uselessly call for actions that government people don't take even with a treaty. At best, treaties are not operational.

At worst, treaties override republican-government safeguards against war.

Forward Basing Doesn't Follow the Constitution

Overrides of the Constitution's mechanisms and of the Constitution's support for common sense are plainly evident with forward basing.

Forward basing initially sounds sensible. Men and materiel will be in place in advance in the event of an attack. If war is started—for example with a surprise attack—the defenders will be better prepared. These advance preparations will even be a deterrent.

NATO

Actually, no. Forward basing accomplishes the opposite, making war not less likely but more likely. Forward basing has four problems.

First, forward basing leads us to rely more on fixed installations. Fixed installations have long proven less valuable than expected in war, and this has long been predictable. Success in war comes from fluid, mobile projection of power. Unpinned from the flawed paradigm of fixed installations, forces would evolve to be more decentralized, lean, mobile, precise, and impactful.

Second, forward basing leads allies to defend themselves less. Each nation's government people act like they consider only their own nation's near-term interests.[15.2, 15.3]

Third, forward basing leads enemies to forward base their own military forces, and to maintain or increase these forces. With their forces in place, possibly enlarged, and ready to be used, enemy government people become more likely to consider attacking. Attacks can increase nationalistic political support. Attacks can opportunistically seize land that has strategic value. Attacks can opportunistically seize people and seize properties that have economic value.

Fourth, forward basing bypasses the constitutional process of declaring and approving war.

15.5

Instead, with forward basing, forces are out there on autopilot, constantly at risk for hostilities, constantly primed for war. If enemy government people move militarily against any nation that has a forward base, we are at significant risk of having our government people not just defend themselves but instead escalate to war reactively, without making a current, deliberate choice. The people won't get current representation in the matter; the choice will have been made in the past by government people, government people who likely aren't subject to ongoing accountability going forward.

War Treaties Don't Follow the Constitution

This fourth issue, bypassing of the accountability of the representatives in each sovereign nation, isn't just a glitch from forward basing; it's a feature of treaties. Treaties' bypassing of sovereign accountability increases treaties' allure to government people. Government people take all kinds of extraordinary measures to shift blame and accountability: for example, unconstitutionally delegating legislative, executive, and judicial powers to administrative agencies, and then turning around and making a show of fighting those agencies on behalf of donors and voters.

Government people use treaties as another such ruse. Once treaties are in place, the bypassing of sovereign accountability is what principally defines how treaties are used in practice.

If a sovereign nation goes to war unilaterally, the government people are politically exposed by having to take a series of actions. The government people buy military equipment, train soldiers, choose rules of engagement, transport equipment and soldiers to foreign soil, declare war, command the forces, and decide the endpoint.

If a nation goes to war under a treaty, the government people are politically shielded by acting as part of a club.[15.4] The actions taken by the club are done as a group. Further, many actions are not taken by any elected members of a national government, but instead are taken by unelected members of the treaty's supranational government. Through these group actions and these delegations of sovereign decisions to supranational rulers, the voters in each individual sovereign nation are denied electoral accountability.

Without the treaty ruse, the electoral accountability available to voters, although small, can exert a sizable impact over time. Voters' principles run deep, especially about wars.[15.5] Challengers who win elections often don't change war policy.

But incumbents facing challengers often do exit wars,[15.6] and this effect compounds over time. In six years, the Iraq coalition declined from 47 nations to 1.

With the treaty ruse, this small but impactful electoral accountability nearly vanishes. Political leaders who credibly could replace current majority leaders or presidents find it less politically attractive to go against the club of a treaty.[15.7] When voters have no alternatives, elections have no consequences. In seventeen years, the Afghanistan coalition of NATO and allies was nearly untouched by public opinion, declining only from 53 nations to 39.[15.8]

War Treaties Create Immoral Wars

This near-zero accountability transmogrifies not just declarations of war but also strategies, operations, and tactics.

War is only moral when it's conducted with care to keep the more-free nation's people safe, and when it's directed at eliminating the offending government and all supplier governments.

When the club of national politicians plans a war, the club delegates the decisionmaking to political appointees, and the political appointees strive to please their patron politicians, the focus is making the politicians sound moral and making the media play nice.

The politicians make it sound moral, even caring, when their political appointees require the use of proportional force. In tactics, don't shoot any enemy person until he first shoots at us or he first acts like he's about to attack us. In operations, target the enemy military people in the field—typically, conscripts—and don't target the enemy-government people responsible for putting our people and theirs at risk. In strategy, stop once the enemy-government people cry "Uncle."

At each level, these appearances of morality deceive; these actions are not moral but immoral. Moral war works the opposite in each case.

In tactics, moral war begins with protecting our own people's safety. For our safety, we must notify the enemy's people in advance that if any of them possess arms or support enemy combatants in any way, we will kill them. We must train our people to kill every enemy person who, by disregarding this fair warning, threatens our safety. We must stand by our people afterwards.

In operations, moral war begins with focusing on eliminating the warmaking government. To eliminate the warmaking government, we must not focus on destroying the enemy's economy,

15.9

the enemy's infrastructure, or even the enemy's conscripts, although we certainly can deceive and destabilize the enemy when helpful. We must always take ground and always hold it. We must as rapidly and decisively as possible take the fight directly to the enemy's civilian or military decisionmakers.

In strategy, moral war begins and ends with eliminating the enemy-government people and their supplier-government people who put our people and their own people at risk in war. To fight war morally, we must always destroy the proven threat to our people. All governments that decide to attack us must be destroyed. All people who consider attacking us in the future must expect to surely lose either their lives or their liberty and property.

NATO Creates Immoral Wars

Moral war destroys the offenders, creating the conditions for extended peace.

Moral peace ensures that the more-free economies grow at their potential rapid rate, so that the more-coercive governments can't win by attacking in war.

NATO lacks this moral mission clarity.

NATO mixes together the most-free, most-peacemaking nations with less-free, less-resolute nations. From the start, the muddied whole is decidedly worse than the sum of its parts.

From there, the parts atrophy under the false security that others will protect them, and that they can get by with doing little to protect themselves if they just go through the motions (including sacrificing some of their people for the club along the way). NATO offers national-government people cover to escape accountability for war. It's an irresistible lure for Progressive national-government people.

In the end, that's what's worst of all. NATO, despite having a record of wars declared, fought, and exited that's dismal, continues to be seen as offering the world's-best insurance against war. By merely existing, through mere longevity, NATO burnishes this reputation. In this way, NATO continues to build up a reputation as the all-time most-functional supranational government.

In government, reputation is power.[15.9] By simply continuing to exist, and by continuing to expand further, NATO threatens every member nation's people, who have better common sense than the people who designed and the people who operate this abomination.

NATO prevents moral war. It reduces moral peace. It kills accountability. And still it expands.

NATO is a sham. All member nations' government people should exit NATO immediately. The United States of America's government people should exit NATO immediately.

rConstitution Paper 16

Failure to Impeach and Convict Denies People Their Rights

PRESIDENTS AND SENATORS *in prior parties have appointed and confirmed judges who have claimed power to decide the constitutionality of laws, and congressmen in prior parties have not impeached and convicted the judges, in defiance of the Constitution.*

Presidents and senators in prior parties have appointed and confirmed judges who have asserted positive rights to compel people to forfeit private property, and congressmen in prior parties have not impeached and convicted the judges, in defiance of the Declaration and the Constitution.

Presidents and senators in prior parties have appointed and confirmed administrators who have committed unconstitutional actions, and congressmen in prior parties have not impeached and convicted the administrators, in defiance of the Constitution.[16.1]

Preventing Losses

Disasters of all kinds stem from multiple smaller problems. A medical error stems from too-few built-in safeguards, too-few informal reviews of other people's work in progress, and some final misstep. A failure of a larger system—a plane crash, a chemical plant disaster—stems from missteps in several areas, which can include design, construction, management, maintenance, and operation. A war or another destructive government action stems from government people piling up errors: inflating money, favoring cronies, disabling customers, enabling enemy-government people. Normal voluntary cooperation suddenly is replaced by a new normal of systematic killing or of depression, with a substantial further step up in government coercion.

Preventing disasters requires preventing multiple problems from building up. This is done by recognizing smaller problems and by addressing each small problem promptly and effectively. Zero tolerance, and no normalizing.

Failure to Impeach and Convict

People in business almost always err at a time when they're trying to add value. A doctor or nurse tries to help a patient. A drug manufacturer's people try to discover harmful side effects. Designers, builders, managers, maintenance people, and operators try to prevent a plane crash, or a chemical plant disaster. In each case, the people responsible bear a burden that is itself quite punishing.

When people erred when they were trying to add value, it's best not to threaten further punishment. Instead, it's best to encourage full disclosure, full understanding of opportunities for prevention, and full communication of lessons learned to people everywhere who do analogous work.

People in government almost always err while they're trying to achieve political objectives. Occasionally these people's actions or inactions respected the Constitution. In this case it's best not to further punish, but rather to learn and to prevent future inadvertent losses.

Increasingly nowadays, though, the government people's actions or inactions will have defied the Constitution. Here, they've proven untrustworthy, and it's best to prevent future defiance and losses.

16.3

Limiting Losses

Regardless of the approach used to prevent future losses, it's always important to limit present losses.

People's losses of rights at the hands of government people are secured against in the Constitution by defining boundaries for government people.

The boundaries are defined in two parts. First, the national-government people in various roles and the state-government people each have certain defined powers, creating separate scopes of operation. Second, the national government's component parts and the state governments have certain other defined powers to oppose others in government in order to push the others back to within the others' scope boundaries.

Securing a role's boundaries requires being faithful to the Constitution regarding both parts of the boundary definition.

The boundary definition's first part, the scope of operation, requires doing two things: First, doing your own job. Second, not doing other people's jobs.

The boundary definition's second part, the opposing powers, requires doing another thing:

Failure to Impeach and Convict

Third, defend your role's boundaries from power grabs by others.

These three requirements run counter to many current elected politicians' incentives and skills. Doing their own jobs means being accountable. Unfortunately, being accountable for things that don't work out well looks bad in reelection campaigns, and lots of things that governments do don't work out well. Even so, it's still feasible to elect some people who will do some portion of their own jobs.

Not doing other people's jobs means having less to take credit for. This looks bad for reelection too. Here too, it's still feasible to elect some people who will not do some portions of other people's jobs.

Defending your job from power grabs by others means sounding less likable. This requirement is particularly hard to fill. It goes against the grain of many elected politicians' best selling point: likeability. Under natural selection, the politicians who survive elections tend to have natural likeability, and also tend to have a natural hunger to be accepted and liked. For most of the natural politicians, fighting off power grabs from others

16.5

would be unnatural. It's hardest to elect people who will defend their role boundaries.

It's up to voters to demand a party that offers candidates who do what's required of them by the Constitution to secure their government role boundaries from other people in the government, which secures people's boundaries from the grabbing hands of the people in the government. When people's boundaries are secure, people's rights as individuals are secure.[16.2]

Using Offsetting Powers

People's present losses of rights as individuals can be limited precisely and quickly by having government people use their offsetting constitutional powers fully.

Various constitutional powers are delegated to government people to limit losses caused by other government people. In most cases there are more than enough powers delegated. Since multiple powers are delegated, even when some government people don't use their constitutional powers, other government people can use other constitutional powers to limit losses.

Failure to Impeach and Convict

As shown in Table 16.1, losses can be routinely stopped by using offsetting powers to control work in process.

Table 16.1. *Offsetting powers in Constitution*[16.3]

Offsetting power (Opportunity)	Clause	Roles offset States	Roles offset Nation Legislative	Roles offset Nation Executive	Roles offset Nation Judicial
Controlling work in process					
National govt. is supreme on delegated powers	VI.2, 10	✓			
Vice president presides over Senate	I.3.4		✓		
Vice president votes in equally-divided Senate	I.3.4		✓		
President objects to bills	I.7.2		✓		
President blocks treaties	II.2.2		✓		
Congress reconsiders bills	I.7.2			✓	
Senate advises, consents on appointments	II.2.2			✓	
Congress makes judicial exceptions, regulations	III.2.2				✓
Congress creates, redesigns inferior courts	I.8.9				✓
Loss limiting by oath to support Constitution					
State executives disregard if unconstitutional	VI.3		✓	✓	✓
President disregards if unconstitutional	II.1.8		✓		✓
President intervenes if unconstitutional	II.1.8	✓			
State legislators disregard if unconstitutional	VI.3		✓	✓	✓
Congresspeople disregard if unconstitutional	VI.3			✓	✓
Congresspeople intervene if unconstitutional	VI.3	✓			
State judges opine	VI.3		✓	✓	✓
National judges opine	III.1, VI.3	✓	✓	✓	
Loss prevention by impeachment					
House impeaches	I.2.5		✓	✓	✓
Senate tries impeachments	I.3.6, I.3.7		✓	✓	✓
Chief justice presides over impeach. trial of pres.	I.3.6				✓

16.7

To offset the legislative branch's powers, the vice president can actively preside over the Senate. He can remove unconstitutional filibuster/cloture and restore constitutional simple-majority voting. This will bring fast change, so good policies achieve maximum impact and bad policies provoke maximum pushback. This great change will also restore the vice president's constitutional power to vote when Senate votes are equally divided.[16.4] Vice presidents have done their jobs in the Senate in the past. They can do their jobs in the Senate at any time now and in the future. When a vice president doesn't use this substantial offsetting power, and the legislation that the president favors doesn't pass the Senate, the president has no grounds for complaining, and playing the victim.

To offset judges' powers, Congress people can make exceptions and regulations. Congress people can also create, redesign, or eliminate all inferior national courts. When Congress people don't use these substantial offsetting powers, and national judges write opinions that Congress people disagree with, Congress people have no grounds for complaining, and playing the victim.

As shown in Table 16.1, present losses can also be limited by using the offsetting power to uphold the oath to support the Constitution.

Failure to Impeach and Convict

By their oaths, attorneys general, governors, and presidents are required to immediately not execute any statues, orders, or opinions, past or present, that they themselves consider unconstitutional. State legislators and Congress people are required to disregard any past statutes, orders, or opinions that they themselves consider unconstitutional. State judges and national judges are required to opine on what they themselves consider unconstitutional.

Nothing ties the hands of any of these officers and forces them to execute, legislate, or opine in any ways that they themselves consider unconstitutional. Quite the reverse. Each of these officers is bound by oath or affirmation to never act in ways that they themselves consider unconstitutional.

And as shown in Table 16.1, future losses can be prevented by impeachment and conviction.

When government people show that they are untrustworthy by violating the Constitution, impeachment is powerful censure, constitutionally moving them to one step away from impeachment conviction. Impeachment conviction and judgment can remove these people immediately and permanently. This offsetting power can immediately prevent new errors. Also, it can bring in new people who permanently eliminate existing errors.

Using Impeachment

The President, Vice President and all civil Officers of the United States, shall be removed from Office on Impeachment for, and Conviction of ...[16.5]

The Senators and Representatives before mentioned, and the Members of the several State Legislatures, and all executive and judicial Officers, both of the United States and of the several States, shall be bound by Oath or Affirmation, to support this Constitution ...[16.6]

The people who can be impeached and convicted are the representatives, senators,[16.7] president, vice president, judges, and all nonmilitary officers. So impeachment and conviction can't be used on national-government officers whose scope is entirely military, but impeachment and conviction can be used on all other national-government officers, from the highest to the lowest.[16.8]

... Treason, Bribery, or other high Crimes and Misdemeanors.[16.9]

The standard for impeachment and conviction is adequately-clear misconduct that suggests that losses will be prevented by not employing a given person anymore now or in the future.[16.10]

Judgment in Cases of Impeachment shall not extend further than to removal from Office, and

Failure to Impeach and Convict

disqualification to hold and enjoy any Office of honor, Trust or Profit under the United States: but the Party convicted shall nevertheless be liable and subject to Indictment, Trial, Judgment and Punishment, according to Law.[16.11]

The President ... shall have Power to grant Reprieves and Pardons for Offences against the United States, except in Cases of Impeachment.[16.12]

Judgments for impeachment conviction prevent future losses due to current office holders or due to future officeholding.

Future losses can and should be prevented all the more swiftly and surely since impeachment-conviction judgments involve not the loss of a right to life, liberty, or property, but rather the loss of a privilege to hold a national-government office.

Most everyone working in the United States is employed at-will.[16.13] Employees are free to leave on their own, and employers are free to dismiss employees for any reason other than race, sex, religion, or national origin.[16.14]

The Constitution creates at-will employment for nonmilitary national-government employees. Impeachment and conviction make sure we have at least one way to dismiss even the most-powerful people who work for us. Government jobs are not entitlements; they're extensions of public trust. When that trust is violated, the privilege of employment should no longer be extended.

Late impeachment prevents future losses by providing judgments that prevent future employment in government positions of trust.

Late impeachment is the only practical way to fully implement these judgments. Late impeachment is needed to make sure that people can't just resign to avoid judgment through impeachment but then later be employed in the national government again.

Late impeachment probably was considered by the Constitution's framers and ratifiers to be well-understood as being the norm. Late impeachment was common practice in England and in states.[16.15] Compared to the impeachment practice prevailing elsewhere at the time, the Constitution explicitly identified a narrower group of people subject to impeachment, a novel process for impeachment, and narrower penalties. The Constitution explicitly added each feature that departed from the prevailing norms, and the Constitution did not explicitly preclude the norm of late impeachment. The most commonsense conclusion is that the Constitution was understood by its framers and ratifiers to delegate power for late impeachment.

16.12

Failure to Impeach and Convict

The sureness of the loss protection provided by impeachment conviction is guaranteed by making the exception of specifically not delegating to presidents the power to pardon impeachment convictions.

> *The House of Representatives ... shall have the sole Power of Impeachment.*[16.16]
>
> *The Senate shall have the sole Power to try all Impeachments. When sitting for that Purpose, they shall be on Oath or Affirmation. When the President of the United States is tried, the Chief Justice shall preside: And no Person shall be convicted without the Concurrence of two thirds of the Members present.*[16.17]

The process of impeachment and conviction should reflect that the individual faces judgments that are decidedly innocuous, and that the public needs protection from losses that are deadly serious.

Impeachment conviction doesn't carry any criminal judgments. Losing a current or future national-government job doesn't ruin a whole life. Even any partial ruination isn't at all caused by the impeachment conviction, it's caused by the adequately-clear misconduct.

The overriding consideration in the impeachment and conviction process therefore needs to be to prevent losses rapidly.

16.13

Preventing losses by protecting the public also is said to be a function of the tort system. The standard in most tort cases—and the standard that, being the most expeditious, should also apply in impeachment and conviction—is a mere preponderance of the evidence. That is, that the weight of the evidence suggesting there was misconduct is at least slightly-more credible than the weight of the evidence suggesting there was not misconduct.[16.18]

This standard is not prescribed by the supreme law, the Constitution.[16.19] The only standard prescribed there is that senators are on oath or affirmation. This calls for each senator to individually perform his or her part in deciding for or against conviction in a manner appropriate to the purpose served by conviction, which, again, is to prevent losses rapidly.

In an ordinary judicial proceeding, a grand jury is constitutionally convened to have citizens weigh all evidence appropriately and decide whether indictment is justified.[16.20] A trial jury of citizens is then protected from possible undue influence by impertinent evidence: for example, hearsay, or negative info on the accused's character.

In an impeachment and impeachment trial, in contrast, the decisions are made by representatives

Failure to Impeach and Convict

and senators. These deciders' very jobs are to create law. Also, in practice these deciders can't be sequestered away from outside influences. Given their work and their political accountability to the people and states they represent, either they can be trusted to weigh evidence appropriately, or at least they've been selected by a process that appears to select people for representatives' and senators' various tasks—including impeachment and conviction—better than any other selection process that's ever been developed.[16.18] As individuals they certainly are more capable, and as a group they likely are more reasonable, than the usual bosses who decide whether to terminate at-will employment for most Americans; and termination of at-will employment, after all, is all that's at stake here for the accused.

Impeachment is a grand-jury action on behalf of the people, conducted by the people's representatives in the House, who decide by a simple-majority vote whether a matter should go to trial.[16.21]

Conviction is a trial action on behalf of the states, conducted by the states' representatives in the Senate, who decide by the votes of a 2/3 majority of the members present whether to convict; whether judgment should include loss of the privilege to hold one's current national-government

16.15

job, if the person currently has one; and whether judgment should include loss of the privilege to hold a national-government job in the future.

The 2/3-majority rule appears to have been a compromise. Above all, it prevents wrongful convictions by factions. Even so, it still enables conviction, for example, if people in the accused person's own faction decide they need to distance themselves from the accused person's adequately-clear misconduct.[16.22]

Zero Tolerance

So much for why to impeach and convict, who, what standard, what judgment, what permanence, when, and how. Next consider how impeachment and conviction would be used if the norm became that government people generally choose to act or to not act in whichever way is needed to support the Constitution.

Ideally, impeachment and conviction would be used every time a person in government defies the Constitution.

People aren't in any way entitled to positions of trust in the government, and people who have defied the Constitution are untrustworthy, so every person who ever defied the Constitution would be

Failure to Impeach and Convict

out. One strike and you're out. Zero tolerance, and therefore zero normalization of deviance. When the backdrop is a norm of trustworthiness, even small deviations become easy to see.

Constitution defiance is highly-visible. Legislators introduce bills to create agencies to which Congress would unconstitutionally delegate legislative power. Executives unconstitutionally command military actions without declarations of war. Judges opine that lives can unconstitutionally be taken away before birth.

These instances of Constitution defiance, and many more such actions or inactions, occur in the public spotlight and can be instantly verified. Investigation amounts to no more than calling up the public record. Logistically, people who act the most unconstitutionally can be summarily impeached and convicted.

Each time misconduct against the Constitution is committed, further losses can be prevented immediately by two quick votes, first in the House and then in the Senate. All in a day's work.

Really, once there's clear documentation that an employee has spent time on the job violating the highest law, what employer would keep the employee for even one more day?

16.17

For the Founders' generation, a rise of taxes to above 2% was enough to call for declaring independence and war.[16.23]

Unfortunately, their robust response to overt coercion by an external ruler wasn't followed by a robust response to smaller incremental coercive steps by internal government people. The Founders and succeeding generations didn't relentlessly impeach and convict Constitution-defying people in government. In the resulting environment of nonzero tolerance, internal coercive actions survived and multiplied.

A starting level of infection can be nearly imperceptible. Even so, even at a small current level of infection, the current size of the infection determines the infection's growth rate. In these conditions, beginning with the tiniest infection and continuing as the infection spreads throughout the environment, the infection level grows exponentially. A growth curve of infection level vs. time looks flat at first, as if nothing's happening. But steadily the growth gathers steam, making the growth curve get steeper and steeper. In the terminal stages, the infection level can't continue increasing exponentially. Resources start getting depleted, and the infection level plateaus. The environment ends up saturated with the infection.

Failure to Impeach and Convict

That's where we are currently with our government's Constitution-defying Progressivism. Throughout the Progressives' century, our two major parties have produced supermajorities of Progressives in every successive Congress.[16.1]

At this point, at the terminal end of more than a century of Progressive monopoly rule, the senators we're stuck with are highly Progressive. For impeachment conviction by 2/3 of senators present, as of this writing the three swing senators would be Christopher Murphy, Tammy Baldwin, and Chris Van Hollen. All are Democrats, with Conservative Review Liberty Scores as low as 9%.[16.24] That score is produced by voting to support the Constitution just 1 time out of 11. To swing the votes of these senators, the misconduct would have to be incredibly gross.

Judges unconstitutionally claiming power to decide the constitutionality of laws, and judges unconstitutionally asserting positive rights to compel people to forfeit private property—such misconduct is exactly what's wanted by these current swing senators.

Individual administrators, though, rank much lower in Progressives' hierarchy for controlling us. Lower administrators are pawns: they're unknown, interchangeable, and much more expendable. If the administrators act visibly enough and unconstitutionally enough, but these swing senators still vote against impeachment convictions, these votes conceivably might cause these swing senators to have trouble getting reelected.

The key to getting started with using impeachment and conviction, like getting started with using any offsetting power against others in government, is to just do it: do the right thing and let the chips fall where they may.

Any time the weight of the evidence suggesting misconduct is at least slightly-more credible than the weight of the evidence suggesting no misconduct, a rapid, simple-majority vote in the House can and should produce impeachment. A rapid 2/3-majority vote of the senators present can then decide conviction.

Further misconduct and losses are guaranteed by inaction or by tortuous, slow investigations skewed towards protecting these untrustworthy employees' supposed privilege to government jobs. But further misconduct and losses are stopped cold by rapid action, repeated as many times as necessary.

For example, when a current Supreme Court majority opines that abortion is constitutional, that

Failure to Impeach and Convict

opinion defies the Constitution by denying the most-fundamental right, the right to life. A simple majority in the House could quickly respond by impeaching the Court's majority en masse based on this Court opinion. Further investigation, evidence, testimony, and procedure would do nothing to offset the weight of this evidence, but instead would just stall, obfuscate, and confuse, all the while enabling ongoing further denials of the right to life.

Conviction votes using the same evidence at the same speed as the impeachments would put senators on record as respecting or denying the right to life.

When these senators sought reelection, the elections would then put voters on record (recorded in each person's memory).

Failing to exercise this impeachment and conviction power to stop abortion denies people their fundamental right to life.

Many national-government officers have similarly committed misconduct that, given modern communications technology, is already well-documented. For example, FBI officers have violated basic procedures, failing to collect evidence and destroying evidence against Hillary Clinton for

16.21

grossly mishandling highly-classified data. IRS officers have broadly denied free-speech rights.

Criminal investigations are warranted in some cases of misconduct. Even so, criminal investigations, prosecutions, and trials that can result in loss of fundamental rights to life, liberty, or property require more care, which takes considerable time. It would be irresponsible to, in the meantime, leave the public exposed to and unprotected from further losses from perpetrators of well-documented misconduct, who are clearly unsuitable for public trust.

Failure to take care to faithfully execute laws is itself misconduct. Failure to fire employees for serious misconduct is also serious executive misconduct. Executives have duties, surely.

But where executives fail, the people are protected solely by Congress's offsetting constitutional power to impeach and convict. Where national-government employees appear to have committed misconduct that makes it risky to keep extending to them further opportunities to cause losses, these employees need to rapidly lose the privilege of working in positions of trust. Congress people have their own independent duty to the people to do their own jobs of impeachment and conviction.

Failure to Impeach and Convict

Progressives Don't Represent Us

Currently, people in the House aren't doing their jobs of impeachment. Every person in the House can be replaced within 2 years. Currently, people in the Senate aren't doing their jobs of impeachment conviction. Every senator can be replaced within 6 years. The Senate's president—the vice president—can be replaced within 4 years.

Currently, such replacements wouldn't change the outcomes. Currently the replacements would come from the two major parties, both of which are majority Progressive. Rather than sending replacements, they would send reinforcements.

But hiding behind a Progressive media as in past years has already become a little more difficult, and it's becoming increasingly difficult.

Theoretically, the Progressives' current lock on the elective offices could be changed internally within one of the two major parties. A persuasive president could encourage new people to come forward, and could encourage the party's people to enact new party rules.

In practice, this Progressive lock on the elective offices can be changed much more readily by developing a new major party.[16.1]

Having government people use their powers against other government people is the only peaceful way to secure people's rights.

Impeachment and conviction is genuine constitutional oversight. It facilitates rapid purging of misconduct to prevent further losses.

A good time to stop further losses is now, from this day forward. The best time to prevent future losses is the first day misconduct is discovered. We the people need Congress people to use their constitutional human-resources power fully. Starting now.

rConstitution Paper 17

Congressional Oversight Is Constitution Defiance

WHEN CONGRESS PEOPLE conduct oversight hearings, this is not responsible government, but the antithesis: a long train of defiances of the Constitution by people in the national government and in the state governments is being approved by the people in the national-government role that has the most power to end the defiance.

Congress people pass laws, presidents execute laws, and judges opine on cases. The greatest power is in the hands of Congress people.

Defiance on War

When Congress people conduct oversight of presidents regarding war, which is a primary area of scope for the national government, Congress people display their approval of a long train of defiances of the Constitution by prior Congress people and by current Congress people.

Increasingly now, war can be prevented. To prevent war best, it's necessary to covertly develop adequate resistance, and to fully respect the Constitution—limiting government—so that people in households and people in business will together build maximum economic strength.

Given adequate resistance and maximum economic strength, all that's required to deter enemy attack is to also always fight war morally, by always destroying the enemy governments. These enemy-government people are the people who threaten our people's lives and their own people's lives in war. Responding by killing is only morally right when our government people are committed to eliminating the threat by destroying those who are morally responsible. This requires that our government people remain committed for the duration of a war. For our government people to remain committed for the duration of a war, our government people must fully respect the Constitution about war.

War must be prepared for by Congress people exercising their exclusive legislative power to make suitable rules of engagement. The rules of engagement must establish conditions during wartime that protect our people, and that ensure that our current technology and forces will destroy the enemy government.

And war must be fought only when Congress people declare war.

Adequate resistance, maximum economic strength, favorable rules of engagement, resolute declarations of war, and certain destruction of enemy governments are what deter enemy-government people from attacking.

Enemy-government people are not deterred by treaties from attacking or dissuaded by treaties from attacking.

With enemy-government people, either a treaty or a collusive unilateral action would increase the power of the enemy-government people, and any increase in their power would increase their likelihood of attacking.

With friendly-government people, any benefit a treaty could provide our nation is better provided by unilateral action. A key example is that when our Congress people unilaterally set zero tariffs on products from the people of friendly nations, this benefits our people, reducing the prices paid by our people both in the short term and in the long run, and increasing the long-term competitiveness of our business people. Our people benefit regardless of whether other nations' government people set tariffs on products, increasing the prices paid by their people.

In general, in the most-consequential matters, the Constitution either enables unilateral action by our national-government people, or in fact requires unilateral action by our national-government people. Our Congress people have sole power to regulate commerce with foreign nations, to make rules of engagement, and to declare war.

Treaties have value for our nation only in the special case when a treaty helps a former enemy nation's government people demonstrate more quickly that they are friendly and they will present a low risk to us if their nation gains full trading benefits more quickly. In this special case, a suitable treaty can let their nation's people bypass the normal wait for their government people to repeatedly demonstrate over time that they are friendly.

So then, the likelihood of war and the outcomes of war are required by the Constitution to be addressed by Congress people's specific actions:

- Covertly developing adequate resistance.

- Constitutionally limiting the government to maximize economic strength.
- Unilaterally and constitutionally setting maximal tariffs and technology-trade restrictions on nations whose government people are enemies.
- Unilaterally and constitutionally setting zero tariffs and technology-trade restrictions on nations whose government people are our friends.
- Making treaties only in unusual special cases in which unilateral action would be slower.
- Unmaking treaties in all other cases.
- Making favorable constitutionally-required rules of engagement.
- Declaring war, as required by the Constitution, and doing it infrequently. This way the economic strength of the people of our more-free nation will increase faster than the economic strength of the people of the more-coercive nations whose government people are our enemies. This will deter those nations' government people from attacking.

Considering the discussion above, clearly Congress people have muscular powers to prevent war.

Clearly, using these actual powers is what Congress people aren't doing when they say they're conducting oversight of presidents regarding war.

The real "oversight" here isn't Congress people's supervision of presidents' actions; it's Congress people's overlooking of Congress people's own inactions: the massive failures by Congress people, past and present, to prevent war by actually using their own muscular constitutional powers.

Defiance on Agencies

When Congress people conduct oversight of agency people regarding agency operations, which are out-of-scope for the national government, Congress people display their approval of long and broad defiances of the Constitution by prior and current people in national and state governments. Including Congress people, naturally.

When government people fully use their constitutional powers against other government people, government people are kept within secure boundaries. Secure boundaries for government people produce secure rights for every individual to keep his own life, liberty, and property. With

Congressional Oversight

secure rights to life, liberty, and property, every individual is free to work with his own talents and networks to add value. When people are free to add value, people add value through activities that, to us, seem most ordinary.

Free people add value by shopping. Shopping brings to the table all that matters to people about their own needs and wants, and all that people know or anticipate about all services and goods available now and in the future. Shopping uses all this understanding, both explicit and tacit, to decide producers' quality, prices, and quantities produced. Ultimately, shopping decides which producers thrive and add more value, which producers add less value, and which producers fail completely.

Free people also add value by working. Working pays costs upfront, designs products, creates production processes, and offers products at proposed levels of quality, price, and quantity.

Freedom is a natural right. Freedom also is a key to our pursuit of happiness, since freedom enables us to best provide for our needs and wants. Mankind's dramatically larger population, longer lives, improved health, and healthier environment[17.1] have all resulted from the United States of America's Constitution initially providing dramatically more-secure freedom from people in government.

Freedom to shop and freedom to work are drastically curtailed, though, when people in government violate the Constitution.

People in government who violate the Constitution suppress free people's abilities to use scarce knowledge, savings, information, and skill to best satisfy all people's needs and wants. Instead, a few government people, using little information, coerce all people to best satisfy the government people's needs and wants.

Government people's unconstitutional coercion has been multiplied in the Progressives' century[17.2] by government agencies. These agencies reintroduced into America the absolute power of kings.[17.3]

All legislative powers granted in the Constitution are vested in Congress.[17.4] Legislation is law. A law is a rule plus a sanction (a threatened penalty).[17.5] No power to issue laws is vested outside Congress. So Congress people act unconstitutionally when they create and leave in place any agencies that create laws—rules and sanctions—through formal rulemaking using hearings; informal rulemaking, skipping hearings; hybrid rulemaking, using added procedures usually added by Congress; very-informal rulemaking, skipping notice and comment by claiming a good cause; negotiated rulemaking, teaming up with cronies in business or in activist groups; standards adoption; interpretation; guidance; best practices; policies; advice; briefs; demands; arm-twisting threats; taxes; tariffs; administrative fees; licensing; waivers; unwritten implicit threats; or further tools-of-the-art.[17.6] All of this lawmaking is unconstitutional. No person in the national government can pass laws constitutionally if the person is not in Congress.

The executive power of the United States of America is vested in a president.[17.7] The executive power in a government has two parts: the offsetting power either to sign or to object to and return Congress's bills that provide supervisory control of revenues and appropriations, and the lead power to manage operations.[17.8, 17.9] Congress people and presidents act unconstitutionally when they create or when they leave in place budgets other than a single top-line budget number and budget targets by high-level division like the divisions of large businesses.[17.8] Setting lower-level budget targets, hiring and terminating employees except as specified in the Constitution, and managing to budget targets are executive powers of presidents alone.

17.9

Congress people and presidents act unconstitutionally when they create or when they leave in place any agencies that manage operations either under the control of Congress people or otherwise outside the control of presidents in any way. No person in the national government can execute laws constitutionally if the person is not under the supervision and control of the president.

The judicial power of the United States is vested in one Supreme Court and in inferior courts ordained and established by Congress. Cases and controversies involving government people start in the Supreme Court, and cases and controversies not involving government people are appealed to the Supreme Court. Exceptions and regulations are made by Congress.[17.10] So Congress people act unconstitutionally when they create and leave in place any agencies that judge laws—rules and sanctions—without constitutional protections: using formal adjudication within the agency, actively seeking out cases, hearing nonstandard evidence, using nonstandard processes, considering "social justice," making determinations, issuing nuisance declarations, assessing penalties, requiring initial appeal inside the agency, influencing outside appeals courts, or using further tools-of-the-art.[17.6, 17.8] No person in the national government can judge cases or controversies constitutionally if the person is not in either the Supreme Court or the inferior courts.

The powers of the states are delegated by the people in their respective states.[17.11] The larger-government Federalists among the Founders anticipated that the people would delegate their respective states powers over militias, local governments, real estate, personal property, domestic affairs, criminal law, civil law for citizens of the same state, religion, education, social services (although mostly provided by churches, families, and communities), agriculture, and other businesses.[17.12] On powers not enumerated to the United States and not prohibited to the states, and therefore reserved to the respective states or reserved to the people, no person in the national government can pass laws, execute laws, or judge cases or controversies constitutionally.[17.11]

Power to push back against others in government is delegated widely to people in government. All legislators, executive civil officers, and judicial officers in the national government and in the state governments are bound by oath or affirmation to support the Constitution.[17.13] Presidents swear or affirm that to the best of their ability they will preserve, protect, and defend the Constitution.[17.14]

17.11

These oaths, at a basic level, are just common sense. Especially in the United States of America, where the sovereign power is openly acknowledged as belonging to individuals, no one in government should violate his conscience by doing anything on the job that he considers illegal because it's unconstitutional. This commonsense principle is simply made explicit through government people's oaths of office.

These oaths can take things to a new level, securing all people's individual rights robustly and resiliently. If government people take their oaths to heart and understand the Constitution passably well, all people's individual rights will be made secure from other government people extremely quickly, and extremely resiliently.

Oaths can secure individuals' rights extremely quickly because every day each government person can take many actions, or can choose inaction, on many tasks. When more of government people's actions or inactions support the Constitution, individuals' rights will immediately be much more secure from government people.

Oaths can secure individuals' rights extremely resiliently because oaths explicitly empower and require everyone in the government to follow the Constitution. This decentralized authority has

Congressional Oversight

always been delegated and entrusted widely to most individuals in the national government and in the state governments, and simply needs to be accepted by one or more of these individuals. Once it is, widespread defiance of the Constitution will be less able to, for example, be initiated with a judicial opinion on a case and then be maintained by unconstitutional inaction by national and state executive officers and legislators. Any single president, any single governor, or any state's legislative majorities will be able to immediately support the Constitution within the sphere of action of each respective individual.

Some power to remove people from the national government resides locally with people in the House and people in the Senate. House members and Senate members may be expelled with the concurrence of two thirds of members of their house.[17.15]

Quite-broad power to remove people from the national government resides with the president. The Constitution directly controls the terms of employment for Congress people, the president, the vice president, and judges, and the hiring of executive officers. All other legislative employees, executive employees, and judicial employees can and should be hired or retained by the president and, when helpful, can and should have their employment terminated by the president. Hiring and terminating employment are executive powers, and the executive power is vested in the president.[17.7, 17.8]

This executive power causes national-government employment other than that of Congress people, the president, the vice president, and judges to be strictly at-will,[17.16] with no exceptions. The president has clear power, and has a clear fiduciary obligation to the people, to only retain an employee if the employee's performance of his job is the best available. At bare minimum, if any employee's past record suggests that he's more likely than a new employee would be to commit future misconduct, the president should quickly revoke such an employee's privilege to work for the government. Not a dime more should be paid to any government employee who threatens the rights of individuals.

This hiring and terminating employment is just human-resources management. To refuse to use this power is to favor one's cronies over one's sovereigns, the people, and to do it right in our faces.

Redundant power to remove people from the national government, together with the additional power to disqualify people from the national government, are conferred by the sole power of impeachment in the House and the sole power of impeachment conviction in the Senate.[17.17, 17.18, 17.19]

Since impeachment and conviction can only limit a defendant's privilege to work in the national government, while impeachment and conviction carry no criminal or civil penalties that would limit a defendant's rights to life or property, the constitutional requirements to be satisfied in impeachment and conviction are quite streamlined. If, taking into account any available evidence of any kind, it seems at least slightly more likely than not that there was misconduct, then to safeguard the rights of individuals from people in the national government, a government person's privileges to possibly commit future misconduct can and should be revoked quickly and permanently.[17.20]

Impeachment and conviction are just supervisory human-resources management. To refuse to use these powers is, again, to favor one's cronies over one's sovereigns, the people, and again, to do it right in our faces.

Progressives in Both Parties

Every national-government agency, by its design or in its operation, violates boundaries set by the Constitution.

Every time an agency's people are brought in for oversight by Congress people, by this action the Congress people reinforce their complicity in the unbroken chain of defiances of the Constitution that enable the agency to exist.

Every agency exists only because Congress people passed a bill; a president signed the bill or Congress people overrode a veto; no judges definitively opined against the statute; no Congress people impeached and convicted the offending Congress people, presidents, and judges; no subsequent presidents refused to execute the statute; and no subsequent Congress people repealed the statute. Every agency that affects a state exists only because no state-government people stopped the resulting statute from being executed in their state.

The many constitutional powers that government people have available to oppose other government people—the powers of people in the national government and in state governments; in legislative, executive, and judicial roles—end up not being used because in all these governments, all these roles are dominated by Progressives.

Progressives are kept in place by both major parties through the parties' candidate-selection processes.

The single best cure is to develop at least one party that has internal self-controls like the national government's internal self-controls provided by the Constitution.

So voters have the real choice they're looking for, to secure our individual rights from foreign government people and from our own government people.[17.21]

rConstitution Paper 18
Nominating Rules for Brand Purity

PEOPLE ADD VALUE BEST when they work together in voluntary cooperation, freely. Our forefathers knew that freedom was greatest when government was limited. Their Constitution provides the necessities: a small scope, independent processes, and offsetting powers. Their parties each rose by promising increased freedom, but then broke bad.

The First Republicans
　　The Republicans of 1792–1825 rose to power as libertarians. In political scope,[18.1] they advocated no treaties, no standing army, no navy, and no wars. In commercial scope,[18.1] they advocated

banking by people in business using gold or silver money certificates, but holding in reserve only enough gold or silver to redeem a small fraction of the paper money's value. They advocated infrastructure development only by people in business.[18.2]

In 1796 the Republicans elected Vice President Thomas Jefferson. In 1800 the Republicans won majorities in Congress and elected President Thomas Jefferson. From there, the Republicans only strengthened further,[18.3] in the end wiping out the Federalists.

But surrounding the war of 1812–1815, the Republicans morphed. In political scope, France and the United Kingdom repeatedly were at war, and the Republicans eventually allowed trade with French people but not with United Kingdom people. The Republicans increased the standing army,[18.4] maintained a small navy,[18.5] and declared war against the United Kingdom.[18.6] In commercial scope, the Republicans not only advocated banking using paper money while holding in reserve only enough gold or silver to redeem a small fraction of the paper money's value, the Republicans also allowed banks to stop redeeming paper money with gold or silver. Soon the Republicans expanded from supporting the

Nominating Rules

war to supporting infrastructure development by people in states.[18.7]

Democrats at First

The Democrats rose to power as relative libertarians. In political scope, they advocated no military treaties, freer-trade commercial treaties,[18.8] a small army, a small navy,[18.9, 18.10] and no wars.[18.11, 18.12] In commercial scope, they advocated banking by people in business using gold or silver money certificates, but holding in reserve only enough gold or silver to redeem a small fraction of the paper money's value.[18.13] They advocated infrastructure development at the national level primarily by people in business,[18.14] but at the state level significantly by people in government.[18.15]

In 1828 the Democrats won majorities in Congress and elected President Andrew Jackson. From there, the Democrats retained control of Congress and the presidency in most elections through 1860, dominating the Whig Party.[18.16]

Even so, the Democrats' planned program of 24 years of libertarian governance under Andrew Jackson, Martin Van Buren, and Thomas Hart Benton[18.2] got broken up halfway in by the panic of 1837 and then the crisis of 1839. In the panic of 1837, England government people's interest rate increases reduced the attractiveness of cotton from America, reducing gold inflow from England. In the crisis of 1839, government people speculated on cotton prices staying high, but cotton prices decreased.

In both cases, prices and money flows decreased. People's wages also decreased, so people stayed employed and were able to buy the same products as before.

But people's loan payments and loan balances didn't also decrease. If people's loan payments and loan balances had also decreased, these decreases would have kept the real values of people's loan payments and loan balances constant, and this would have kept people's property rights secure. Instead, since the nominal amounts of people's loan payments and loan balances stayed constant, the real values of people's loan payments and loan balances increased. Some people failed to make the higher real-value loan payments. Other people tried to withdraw their money from banks to cover the higher real-value loan payments, and because of this, many banks failed. Altogether, many borrowers, savers, and investors suffered big losses.[18.13]

All this could have been prevented.

18.4

Nominating Rules

A fundamental protection of property rights would have been to require that money be backed 100% by reserves that either retained their value or increased in value. This would have prevented some crises by preventing lending to borrowers who were more likely to fail. When crises did happen, this would have reduced the crises' severity. And during crises, this would have fully protected people who deposited in banks and people who invested in banks.

A further protection of property rights, in this case protecting people who borrowed, would have been to adjust nominal loan payments and loan balances to keep the real values of loan payments and loan balances constant.

The Democrats' libertarian policies would have advanced further if government people had simply followed through on the Constitution's protection of property rights. If they had simply focused on first principles.

Republicans

The current Republicans rose to power as relative libertarians in one defining policy: abolition of slavery, securing black individuals' natural right to liberty.[18.17]

18.5

In 1854 and 1858 the Republicans won majorities in the House. In 1860 the Republicans won majorities in Congress and elected President Abraham Lincoln. From there, the Republicans retained control of Congress and the presidency through 1872.[18.16]

Secession and Civil War removed the Southern voters. When peace was reached, the abolition of slavery realigned the Southern voters at first. But the abolition of slavery had also removed the new Republicans' sole policy that was libertarian.

Democrats Postwar

After the abolition of slavery made slavery no longer an issue, the Democrats became the relative libertarians again, advocating smaller, less-coercive government, and the Democrats became competitive again.

In 1874 the Democrats won the majority in the House, and they kept that majority for most of the next 20 years. In 1884 they also elected President Grover Cleveland. In 1888 they were swept out, but in 1892 they won majorities in Congress and again elected President Cleveland.[18.16]

And then once again the Democrats were ripped by back-to-back panics, in 1893 and in 1896.

Nominating Rules

The panic of 1893 was due to the Republicans increasing tariffs to increase government spending, and due to the Republicans inflating the quantity of paper money (by buying silver using inflated paper money), changing New York customs payments from being in gold to being in inflated paper money, and muscling New York banks to sell back their gold in exchange for inflated paper money. Incoming Democratic President Cleveland ended the inflation of the quantity of paper money by ending the silver purchases, which restored the confidence of people in business temporarily. Unfortunately this wasn't enough to keep a relatively-libertarian major party available to voters. In 1894 a Democratic faction, that, like the Republicans, also favored inflationary policies, took over the Democratic Party. Even though the new Democratic faction lost both houses of Congress in that election, the new Democratic faction still controlled the party from then on.

The panic of 1896 was due to the Democrats nominating a new Democratic candidate for president who advocated substantial use of silver-backed currency,[18.18] inflating the quantity of money. Savers began withdrawing their money in the form of gold, drawing gold reserves down, which pushed prices down. The Republicans immediately seized

18.7

on a new way to add voters to their big-government coalition by brazenly flipping on a longstanding major policy, becoming the party that advocated money that would be less inflationary because it was at least fractionally backed by gold.

Suddenly, and from then on, neither major party was relatively libertarian. Both major parties favored an unconstitutional high-spending, coercive national government.[18.19]

With voters denied candidates who would make a meaningful difference, in less than a generation the resulting voter powerlessness took a substantial toll. From 1896 to 1912, turnout plummeted from 79% to 59%. In just 16 years, the proportion of people voting had fallen by 25%. Since then, although turnout has occasionally recovered slightly to 63%, turnout has mostly declined further, to as low as 49%.[18.20]

Crisis and Leviathan[18.21]

This history reveals important patterns.

The party that advocates more freedom from coercion by government people was always more popular in the long run. The party that advocated the most freedom from coercion by government people, the Republican Party of 1792–1825, was the most popular.

Nominating Rules

But no parties have ever acted quickly to fully secure people from war and to fully secure people's property rights from destructive losses stemming from money not being backed 100% by gold or silver reserves. Unconstitutional use of fractional-reserve paper money has always been followed by changes in the quantity of money with no corresponding changes in nominal loan balances and payments. This has meant that real loan balances and payments have increased, hitting borrowers with sudden, substantial losses. (Lenders have gained corresponding sudden windfalls, but lenders have not relieved borrowers' losses.) These losses have further caused runs on banks, causing banking suspensions or bank failures, hitting borrowers, savers, and investors with more losses.

As a result of parties' failures to fully secure people from war and to fully secure people's property rights from money not backed 100% by gold or silver reserves, a major war or a major peacetime economic loss has always come fast enough to create temporary political openings for parties that increase coercion by government, reducing freedom.

It hasn't mattered which party gained power. No parties have been internally secured to keep

18.9

them from morphing to end up increasing coercion by government, taking away freedom. Every party has been unsecured, and every party has morphed.

This history shows that there's a huge opportunity here for a party that advocates more freedom from coercion by government people, that acts quickly enough to fully secure people from war and to fully secure people's property rights from money not backed 100% by gold or silver reserves, and that's internally secured so that it keeps advocating more freedom from coercion by government people.

The Constitution for Crisis Prevention

The best-available process for securing freedom from coercion by government people is to have government people fully use the powers delegated to them through the Constitution to oppose other government people.[18.1]

The quickest-available process to fully secure people from war is to repeal all statutes that expand the national and state governments beyond the scopes enumerated in the national and state constitutions—so that the national and state governments immediately shrink down to the minimal size needed to prevent overrun by enemies and to otherwise secure the sovereign individual people's natural rights to life, liberty, and property—and then stay out of the way.

Allowing people to work together freely, using the best of their abilities to add value, builds economic strength faster than enemies can build economic strength. This economic strength at minimum wins wars.

When allowed to proceed over longer time periods, this economic strength can so overwhelm potential enemy-government people that they will not attack in the first place in ways that threaten our existence, because they reasonably expect that we would survive, counterattack, and destroy the enemy government, including them.

And if we disincentivize potential enemy-government people from threatening us, eventually their nations will do the rest that's needed to change by themselves. Either their government people will relent and increase freedom, or the people themselves will replace their government people with new people who will increase freedom.[18.22]

The best-available process to fully secure people's property rights from money not backed 100% by gold or silver reserves is to repeal all statutes that unconstitutionally favor paper money or that depend on the quantity of paper money getting inflated.

18.11

Simply put, the best way to secure individuals from losing some of their property due to paper money is to use constitutional money:

1. Allow gold to be used as money (as explicitly mentioned in the Constitution),[18.23] by repealing laws that interfere, including investment taxes.[18.24]

2. Allow equities (common stocks, which are shares in ownership of companies) and equity funds (mutual funds that hold equities) to be used as money,[18.25] by repealing laws that interfere, including investment taxes and reporting requirements.

3. Disallow all unconstitutional features of our paper monetary system (to fulfill the aspirational proscription against paper money in the Constitution,[18.23] and to secure people's rights to keep their own property as required by the Constitution).[18.26, 18.27]

    3.1 Repeal the legal tender laws on paper money, so people are no longer forced to accept paper money.[18.28]

    3.2 Repeal all laws enabling banking and insurance to be controlled by government and government cronies. End the Fed (government control of the

Nominating Rules

quantity of money);[18.29] Fannie Mae and Freddie Mac (government control of lending to real estate buyers);[18.30] Sallie Mae (government lending for higher education); FDIC and FSLIC, NFIP, and FCIC (government insurance of banking, flood risk, and crop risk); and the like.

3.3 End government inflation of the quantity of paper money.[18.25]

3.4 Repeal all laws controlling lending (including laws that stop business people from controlling their risks).[18.30]

3.5 Repeal all laws allowing banks to inflate the quantity of paper money by lending using fractional reserves.[18.25] If a bank makes any new loans based on fractional reserves—that is, if the bank makes any new loans that exceed the new savings deposited—take care to faithfully execute the law[18.31] by prosecuting this money creation as fraud.[18.32]

3.6 Repeal all laws that substitute for investment, banking, and insurance, particularly laws on government-

18.13

controlled retirement income and laws enabling government and government-crony medical payments.[18.33] Fund all liabilities promised so far to people in the current system by selling existing assets, and by delivering these assets to the people themselves, so the people themselves can control these assets going forward.[18.34]

A New Party Design

To get all this unconstitutional government scope repealed, we the people need to select candidates for elected representative offices who will follow the Constitution. To do this we will need a robust set of controls, provided by a new party.

The determination that the party's people will follow the Constitution as written, as explained by Randy Barnett in *Our Republican Constitution*, should be asserted with a meaningful party name:
republican Constitution party

The way the government is designed to work, the actions needed from government people to make the government work as designed, and the

Nominating Rules

consequences of failure to take these actions should be explained in the party declaration's preamble:

Our life, liberty, property rights, and supporting rights are made secure from government people through the Constitution separating the state, legislative, executive, and judicial powers, through the Constitution defining offsetting powers, and through government people respecting other government people's powers and asserting their own offsetting powers. When government people fail to respect others' powers or when government people fail to assert their own offsetting powers, government people deny us our rights.

A party structure and the party's supreme laws, both of which keep the party's grassroots voters solidly in control, and both of which facilitate robust selection of candidates who will follow the Constitution, should be set out in the party constitution:

[The] congress of the republican Constitution party ... shall have power to solicit and collect donations;

to arrange national party meetings;

18.15

> to set schedules for, and national party controls on, state party selection of candidates for the national government …
>
> [The] president of the republican Constitution party … shall have power, by and with the advice and consent of the senate, to make party-sanctioned debate schedules, provided two thirds of the senators concur.
>
> The republican Constitution party shall have no platform.

The party's constitution should also replicate other parts of the nation's Constitution that have analogies for a party: further applicable parts of Articles I, II, and III regarding legislative, executive, and judicial powers; applicable parts of Articles IV, V, VI, and VII regarding states, amendment, supreme law, and ratification; and applicable parts of Amendments 10, 12, 17, 22, 23, and 26 regarding state powers, presidential election, election of senators, presidential term limits, DC electors, and voting age.

Further rules, which let the grassroots' party-government representatives make limited adjustments to the processes and metrics used to select candidates, should be set out in the party laws:

A previously-elected candidate shall qualify to run as a member of the party only if his Conservative Review Liberty Score is a minimum of 80%.

Party-sanctioned debates shall have no moderators, no commentators from the start to the finish of the debate, and no questions other than the questions asked by the candidates during the debates.

Candidates for Congress shall be selected using closed caucuses with proportional voting.

The candidate for president shall be selected using closed caucuses with proportional voting, using a candidate electoral college the same in numbers and distribution as the electoral college, and counting only candidate electors from regions represented by the party in the House or Senate.

State caucuses to select candidates for Congress and president shall be scheduled one state at a time, approximately equally-spaced apart in time, in order of decreasing party strength. The party strength shall be the average of the party proportions of the vote in the most-recent elections for each

House and Senate seat in the state, with each election counted as being of equal weight in the average.[18.35]

Only a Party Has Enough Control Power

The Constitution is the best-available design to keep individuals' liberties secure from government people. This design works only if government people exercise their power to oppose other government people.

Parties have the control power to determine whether government people use their power to secure the people's liberties. Personnel is policy.

Past party designs have enabled parties to select representatives who enact changes too slowly to prevent future crises: wars, or peacetime economic losses due to government actions. Crises make conditions ripe to circumvent the Constitution to grow government, reducing liberty.

Past party designs have further failed to stop parties from having shifts in their majority coalitions that flip the parties' majority character. These flips have always moved the parties towards coercion, and these flips have never been reversed to move the parties back towards liberty. (When voters elected a more-constitutionalist president like Reagan, and when voters elected more-constitutionalist minorities of representatives and senators during the Obama years, the overall change in statutes and regulations continued to be towards increasing coercion. For the overall change to be towards increasing liberty, voters would have to elect more-constitutionalist majorities of representatives and senators.)

With a party-government design like the government design in the Constitution, the party's grassroots people will finally have supervisory control over candidate selection. With the grassroots controlling the party, the party will select candidates who will use their constitutional powers to oppose other government people. These candidates are popular and will be elected.[18.36]

Right here, right now, we can achieve a giant step up in freedom.

The Constitution offers us processes that are proven at full scale. We can readily scale down these processes to build a better party. And it has turned out that the parties are the tails that wag the dog. The parties are the controls.

Upgrade the controls, and the Constitution's processes will make individuals' liberties secure.

References

1.1 De Soto, Hernando. "Listening to the Barking Dogs: Property Law against Poverty in the Non-West." *Focaal: European Journal of Anthropology*, no. 41, 2003, pp. 179–86.

1.2 Kanngiesser, Patricia, and Bruce M. Hood. "Young Children's Understanding of Ownership Rights for Newly Made Objects." *Cognitive Development*, vol. 29, no. 1, 2014, pp. 30–40.

1.3 Bolton, Robert. *People Skills*. Touchstone, 2009, pp. 262–314.

1.4 Rothbard, Murray N. *The Progressive Era*. Edited by Patrick Newman, Mises Institute, 2017, pp. 163–97.

1.5 Trumbull, Robert. "Japan Welcomes Eban Warmly: Her Industry Impresses Israeli." *New York Times*, 19 Mar. 1967, p. 14, quoteinvestigator.com/2012/11/11/exhaust-alternatives/. Accessed 13 June 2017.

1.6 "Fannie Mae." *Wikipedia*, 9 May 2017, en.wikipedia.org/wiki/Fannie_Mae. Accessed 16 June 2017.

[1.7] "Freddie Mac." *Wikipedia*, 10 May 2017, en.wikipedia.org/wiki/Freddie_Mac. Accessed 16 June 2017.

[1.8] Neilsen, Barry. "Fannie Mae and Freddie Mac, Boon or Boom?" *Investopedia*, www.investopedia.com/articles/07/fannie-freddie.asp. Accessed 16 June 2017.

[1.9] Wallison, Peter J. *Dissent from the Majority Report of the Financial Crisis Inquiry Commission*. American Enterprise Institute for Public Policy Research, 2011, pp. 10–5.

[1.10] "James Madison." *Wikipedia*, 13 June 2017, en.wikipedia.org/wiki/James_Madison. Accessed 13 June 2017.

[1.11] "Montpelier: The People, The Place, The Idea." www.montpelier.org/the-story-of-montpelier. Accessed 19 June 2017.

[1.12] "Gouverneur Morris." *Wikipedia*, 8 May 2017, en.wikipedia.org/wiki/Gouverneur_Morris. Accessed 19 June 2017.

[1.13] Lindert, Peter H., and Jeffrey G. Williamson. "American Colonial Incomes, 1650–1774." *The Economic History Review*, vol. 69, no. 1, 2016, pp. 54–77.

References

2.1 "List of United States Presidential Elections by Electoral College Margin." *Wikipedia*, 13 June 2017, en.wikipedia.org/wiki/List_of_United_States_presidential_elections_by_Electoral_College_margin. Accessed 28 June 2017.

2.2 Ferling, John. *The Ascent of George Washington: The Hidden Political Genius of an American Icon.* Bloomsbury Press, 2010, p. xxi.

2.3 Ferling, John. *The Ascent of George Washington: The Hidden Political Genius of an American Icon.* Bloomsbury Press, 2010, p. 368.

2.4 Harrison, Adrienne Marie. *"His Mind Was Great and Powerful": George Washington's Reading and the Fashioning of His American Self.* Dissertation, Rutgers University, 2013.

2.5 "George Washington." *Wikipedia*, 5 July 2017, en.wikipedia.org/wiki/George_Washington. Accessed 5 July 2017.

2.6 Ferling, John. *The Ascent of George Washington: The Hidden Political Genius of an American Icon.* Bloomsbury Press, 2010, pp. 368–9.

2.7 Lindert, Peter H., and Jeffrey G. Williamson. *Unequal Gains: American Growth and Inequality Since 1700.* EPUB version, Princeton University Press, 2016, p. 62.

2.8 Stewart, David O. *The Summer of 1787: The Men Who Invented the Constitution.* Simon and Schuster, 2008, pp. 1–10.

2.9 Phelps, Glenn A. *George Washington and American Constitutionalism*. University Press of Kansas, 1993, pp. 192–3.

2.10 Harrison, Adrienne Marie. *"His Mind Was Great and Powerful": George Washington's Reading and the Fashioning of His American Self.* Dissertation, Rutgers University, 2013, pp. 291–7.

2.11 Morrison, Jeffry H. *The Political Philosophy of George Washington*. Johns Hopkins University Press, 2009, pp. 16–8.

2.12 Evans, Thomas W. *The Education of Ronald Reagan: The General Electric Years and the Untold Story of His Conversion to Conservatism*. Columbia University Press, 2006.

References

3.1 USA Declaration of Independence, 1776.

3.2 USA Constitution, amend. 9.

3.3 Lindert, Peter H., and Jeffrey G. Williamson. "American Colonial Incomes, 1650–1774." *The Economic History Review*, vol. 69, no. 1, 2016, pp. 54–77.

3.4 USA Constitution, art. VI, cl. 3.

3.5 Story, Joseph. *Commentaries on the Constitution of the United States: With a Preliminary Review of the Constitutional History of the Colonies and States before the Adoption of the Constitution*. 4th ed., with notes and additions, vol. I, Boston, Little, Brown, and Company, 1873, p. 265.

3.6 Relyea, Harold C. "The Law: The Executive Office of the Vice President: Constitutional and Legal Considerations." *Presidential Studies Quarterly*, vol. 40, no. 2, 2010, pp. 327–41.

3.7 Coenen, Dan T. "The Filibuster and the Framing: Why the Cloture Rule Is Unconstitutional and What to Do about It." *Boston College Law Review*, vol. 55, no. 1, 2014, pp. 39–92.

3.8 Lebel, C., et al. "Microstructural Maturation of the Human Brain from Childhood to Adulthood." *Neuroimage*, vol. 40, no. 3 (2008), pp. 1044–55.

3.9 Lebel, Catherine, and Christian Beaulieu. "Longitudinal Development of Human Brain Wiring Continues from Childhood into Adulthood." *The Journal of Neuroscience*, vol. 31, no. 30, 2011, pp. 10937–47.

4.1 Anthony, James. *The Constitution Needs a Good Party: Good Government Comes from Good Boundaries.* Neuwoehner Press, 2018.

4.2 "Law." *Merriam-Webster,* www.merriam-webster.com/dictionary/law. Accessed 16 Aug. 2017.

4.3 "Sanction." *Google,* www.google.com/search?q=sanction&oq=sanction&gs_l=psy-ab.3..0i67k1j0j0i131k1l2.16085.17046.0.17280.8.6.0.0.0.0.234.234.2-1.1.0....0...1.1.64.psy-ab..7.1.234.krqgxUun79g. Accessed 16 Aug. 2017.

4.4 "Who Writes Our Law?" *GovTrack.us,* 24 Mar. 2010, govtracknews.wordpress.com/2010/03/24/who-writes-our-law/. Accessed 31 July 2017.

4.5 Pierce, Richard J., Jr. "Seven Ways to Deossify Agency Rulemaking." *Administrative Law Review,* vol. 47, 1995, pp. 59–95; p. 85.

4.6 Wayne Crews, Clyde, Jr. *Mapping Washington's Lawlessness.* Competitive Enterprise Institute, 2017, pp. 40–4.

4.7 Eastwood, Clint, actor. *Magnum Force.* The Malpaso Company, 1973.

4.8 Adams, Rick A., et al. "Predictions Not Commands: Active Inference in the Motor System." *Brain Structure and Function,* vol. 218, no. 3, 2013, pp. 611–43.

4.9 Bargh, J. A., and T. L. Chartrand. "The Unbearable Automaticity of Being." *American Psychologist,* vol. 54, no. 7, 1999, pp. 462–79.

References

4.10 Nation, Paul. "Reading Faster." *International Journal of English Studies*, vol. 9, no. 2, 2009, pp. 131–45.

4.11 Pfeiffer, Michelle, actress. *Scarface*. Universal Pictures, 1983.

4.12 Bommarito, Michael J., and Daniel M. Katz. "A Mathematical Approach to the Study of the United States Code." *Physica A: Statistical Mechanics and Its Applications*, vol. 389, no. 19, 2010, pp. 4195–200.

4.13 McLaughlin, Patrick. "The Code of Federal Regulations: The Ultimate Longread." *Mercatus*, George Mason University Mercatus Center, 1 Apr. 2015, www.mercatus.org/publication/code-federal-regulations-ultimate-longread-game-thrones-hunger-games. Accessed 5 June 2019.

4.14 Henchman, Joseph. "How Many Words Are in the Tax Code?" *Tax Foundation*, 15 Apr. 2014, taxfoundation.org/how-many-words-are-tax-code. Accessed 21 Aug. 2017.

4.15 Uvnäs-Moberg, Kerstin. "Oxytocin May Mediate the Benefits of Positive Social Interaction and Emotions." *Psychoneuroendocrinology*, vol. 23, no. 8, 1998, pp. 819–35.

4.16 Irving, Washington. *Rip Van Winkle*. Philadelphia, Henry Altemus, 1896.

4.17 Center for Chemical Process Safety (CCPS). *Layer of Protection Analysis: Simplified Process Risk Assessment*. Wiley, 2001.

4.18 Hamburger, Philip. *The Administrative Threat*. Encounter Books, 2017.

4.19 USA Constitution, art. I, sec. 1.

4.20 USA Constitution, art. VI, cl. 3.

4.21 USA Constitution, art. II, sec. 1, cl. 1.

4.22 McLaughlin, Patrick A., and Oliver Sherouse. "RegData US." *QuantGov,* Mercatus Center at George Mason University, 2019, quantgov.org/regdata-us/. Accessed 22 June 2019. RegData US 3.1 Annual Summary dataset.

References

5.1 Anthony, James. *The Constitution Needs a Good Party: Good Government Comes from Good Boundaries.* Neuwoehner Press, 2018.

5.2 Cook, Claire Kehrwald. *The MLA's Line by Line: How to Edit Your Own Writing.* Houghton Mifflin, 1985, pp. 1–17.

5.3 Strunk, William, Jr. *The Elements of Style.* Harcourt, Brace and Company, 1920, pp. 24–5.

5.4 Galbraith, David. "Writing as a Knowledge-Constituting Process." *Knowing What to Write: Conceptual Processes in Text Production,* edited by Mark Torrance and David Galbraith, Amsterdam University, 1999, pp. 139–64.

5.5 "Law." *Merriam-Webster,* www.merriam-webster.com/dictionary/law. Accessed 16 Aug. 2017.

5.6 "Sanction." *Google,* www.google.com/search?q=sanction&oq=sanction&gs_l=psy-ab.3..0i67k1j0j0i131k1l2.16085.17046.0.17280.8.6.0.0.0.0.234.234.2-1.1.0....0...1.1.64.psy-ab..7.1.234.krqgxUun79g. Accessed 16 Aug. 2017.

5.7 Epstein, Richard Allen. *Simple Rules for a Complex World.* Harvard University Press, 1995, p. 308.

5.8 USA Constitution, art. II, sec. 1, cl. 1.

5.9 Reid, R. Dan, and Nada R. Sanders. *Operations Management: An Integrated Approach.* 5th ed., Wiley, 2013, p. 2.

5.10 USA Constitution, art. I, sec. 8, cl. 1.

5.11 USA Constitution, art. I, sec. 9, cl. 7.

[5.12] United States, Government Accountability Office, Office of the General Counsel. *Principles of Federal Appropriations Law*. 4th ed., Government Printing Office, 2016, p. 2–11.

[5.13] McClanahan, Brion. *The Founding Fathers' Guide to the Constitution*. Regnery History, 2012.

[5.14] USA Constitution, art. III, sec. 1.

[5.15] USA Constitution, art. III, sec. 2, cl. 2.

[5.16] USA Constitution, art. III, amends. 4–8.

[5.17] Postell, Joseph. *From Administrative State to Constitutional Government*. The Heritage Foundation, 2012, pp. 16–9.

[5.18] Epstein, Richard Allen. *Simple Rules for a Complex World*. Harvard University Press, 1995.

References

6.1 Anthony, James. *The Constitution Needs a Good Party: Good Government Comes from Good Boundaries.* Neuwoehner Press, 2018.

6.2 USA Constitution, art. I, sec. 1.

6.3 USA Constitution, art. I, sec. 3, cl. 1.

6.4 USA Constitution, amend. 17, cl. 1.

6.5 USA Constitution, art. I, sec. 2, cl. 3.

6.6 Manin, Bernard. *The Principles of Representative Government.* Cambridge University Press, 1997, p. 130.

6.7 Barnett, Randy E. *Our Republican Constitution: Securing the Liberty and Sovereignty of We the People.* Broadside Books, 2016, p. 252.

6.8 "Law." *Merriam-Webster,* www.merriam-webster.com/dictionary/law. Accessed 16 Aug. 2017.

6.9 "Sanction." *Google,* www.google.com/search?q=sanction&oq=sanction&gs_l=psy-ab.3..0i67k1j0j0i131k1l2.16085.17046.0.17280.8.6.0.0.0.0.234.234.2-1.1.0....0...1.1.64.psy-ab..7.1.234.krqgxUun79g. Accessed 16 Aug. 2017.

6.10 Schoenbrod, David. "Goal Statutes or Rules Statutes: The Case of the Clean Air Act." *UCLA Law Review,* vol. 30, 1982, pp. 740–828.

6.11 Hargadon, Andrew B. "Firms as Knowledge Brokers: Lessons in Pursuing Continuous Innovation." *California Management Review,* vol. 40, no. 3, 1998, pp. 209–27.

[6.12] Hamburger, Philip. *Is Administrative Law Unlawful?* EPUB version, University of Chicago Press, 2014, pp. 165–89.

[6.13] Wayne Crews, Clyde, Jr. *Mapping Washington's Lawlessness.* Competitive Enterprise Institute, 2017, pp. 36–7.

[6.14] Anderson, Heather. "UDAAP Enforcement the Next Big Threat." *Credit Union Times,* 29 July 2015.

[6.15] Wayne Crews, Clyde, Jr. *Mapping Washington's Lawlessness.* Competitive Enterprise Institute, 2017, p. 41.

[6.16] Schneider, Benjamin. "The People Make the Place." *Personnel Psychology,* vol. 40, no. 3, 1987, pp. 437–53.

[6.17] Kibbe, Matt. *Hostile Takeover: Resisting Centralized Government's Stranglehold on America.* Harper Collins, 2012, p. xii.

[6.18] Mares, Jan. "25 Differences between Private Sector and Government Managers." *Power,* May 2013.

[6.19] D'Emidio, Tony, et al. "Improving the Customer Experience to Achieve Government-Agency Goals." *McKinsey & Company,* Feb. 2017, www.mckinsey.com/industries/public-sector/our-insights/improving-the-customer-experience-to-achieve-government-agency-goals. Accessed 12 Sep. 2017.

[6.20] Nugent, Ted. *Cat Scratch Fever.* Epic, 1977.

[6.21] USA Constitution, art. II, sec. 1, cl. 1.

6.22 USA Constitution, art. VI, cl. 3.

6.22 USA Constitution, art. II, sec. 1, cl. 8.

6.24 Story, Joseph. *Commentaries on the Constitution of the United States: With a Preliminary Review of the Constitutional History of the Colonies and States before the Adoption of the Constitution*. 4th ed., with notes and additions, vol. I, Boston, Little, Brown, and Company, 1873, p. 265.

7.1 Anthony, James. *The Constitution Needs a Good Party: Good Government Comes from Good Boundaries.* Neuwoehner Press, 2018.

7.2 USA Constitution, amend. 5.

7.3 USA Declaration of Independence, 1776.

7.4 Epstein, Richard Allen. *Simple Rules for a Complex World.* Harvard University Press, 1995, pp. 219–24.

7.5 Ma, Philip, and Rodney Zemmel. "Value of Novelty?" *Nature Reviews Drug Discovery,* vol. 1, no. 8, 2002, pp. 571–3.

7.6 Light, Donald W., and Joel R. Lexchin. "Pharmaceutical Research and Development: What Do We Get for All That Money?" *BMJ,* vol. 345, no. e4348, 2012, pp. 1–5.

7.7 Peltzman, Sam. "An Evaluation of Consumer Protection Legislation: The 1962 Drug Amendments." *Journal of Political Economy,* vol. 81, no. 5, 1973, pp. 1049–91.

7.8 Higgs, Robert. "Banning a Risky Product Cannot Improve Any Consumer's Welfare (Properly Understood), with Applications to FDA Testing Requirements." *The Review of Austrian Economics,* vol. 7, no. 2, 1994, pp. 3–20.

7.9 Miller, James. *Statement of FDA Mission.* 2012.

7.10 Rumsfeld, Donald H. "DoD News Briefing—Secretary Rumsfeld and Gen. Myers." *archive.defense.gov,* 12 Feb. 2002, archive.defense.gov/Transcripts/Transcript.aspx?TranscriptID=2636. Accessed 12 Feb. 2019.

References

[7.11] Carpenter, Daniel, and Gisela Sin. "Policy Tragedy and the Emergence of Regulation: The Food, Drug, and Cosmetic Act of 1938." *Studies in American Political Development*, vol. 21, no. 2, 2007, pp. 149–80.

[7.12] Ballentine, Carol. "Taste of Raspberries, Taste of Death: The 1937 Elixir Sulfanilamide Incident." *FDA Consumer Magazine*, vol. 15, no. 5, June 1981.

[7.13] Sherman, Max, and Steven Strauss. "Thalidomide: A Twenty-Five Year Perspective." *Food, Drug, Cosmetic Law Journal*, vol. 41, 1986, pp. 458–66.

[7.14] Shorter, Edward. "The Liberal State and the Rogue Agency: FDA's Regulation of Drugs for Mood Disorders, 1950s–1970s." *International Journal of Law and Psychiatry*, vol. 31, no. 2, 2008, pp. 126–35.

[7.15] Tabarrok, Alexander T. "Assessing the FDA via the Anomaly of Off-Label Drug Prescribing." *The Independent Review*, vol. 5, no. 1, 2000, pp. 25–53.

[7.16] Dickson, Michael, and Jean Paul Gagnon. "Key Factors in the Rising Cost of New Drug Discovery and Development." *Nature Reviews Drug Discovery*, vol. 3, no. 5, 2004, pp. 417–29.

[7.17] Adams, Christopher P., and Van V. Brantner. "Estimating the Cost of New Drug Development: Is It Really $802 Million?" *Health Affairs*, vol. 25, no. 2, 2006, pp. 420–8.

[7.18] Light, Donald W., and Rebecca Warburton. "Demythologizing the High Costs of Pharmaceutical Research." *BioSocieties*, vol. 6, no. 1, 2011, pp. 34–50.

7.19 Peltzman, Sam. *Regulation of Pharmaceutical Innovation: The 1962 Amendments.* American Enterprise Institute for Public Policy Research, 1974, p. 13.

7.20 Klein, Daniel B., and Alexander Tabarrok. "Theory, Evidence and Examples of FDA Harm." *FDA Review.org, a Project of the Independent Institute,* 2016, www.fdareview.org/issues/theory-evidence-and-examples-of-fda-harm/. Accessed 25 Sep. 2017.

7.21 DiMasi, Joseph A., and Henry G. Grabowski. "Should the Patent System for New Medicines Be Abolished?" *Clinical Pharmacology & Therapeutics,* vol. 82, no. 5, 2007, pp. 488–90.

7.22 Peltzman, Sam. "Regulation and the Natural Progress of Opulence." *Economic Affairs,* vol. 30, no. 2, June 2010, pp. 33–9.

7.23 Darrow, Jonathan J. "Pharmaceutical Efficacy: The Illusory Legal Standard." *Washington and Lee Law Review,* vol. 70, no. 4, 2013, pp. 2073–136.

7.24 Carpenter, Daniel P. "The Political Economy of FDA Drug Review: Processing, Politics, and Lessons for Policy." *Health Affairs,* vol. 23, no. 1, 2004, pp. 52–63.

7.25 "Law." *Merriam-Webster,* www.merriam-webster.com/dictionary/law. Accessed 16 Aug. 2017.

7.26 "Sanction." *Google,* www.google.com/search?q=sanction&oq=sanction&gs_l=psy-ab.3..0i67k1j0j0i131k1l2.16085.17046.0.17280.8.6.0.0.0.0.234.234.2-1.1.0....0...1.1.64.psy-ab..7.1.234.krqgxUun79g. Accessed 16 Aug. 2017.

References

8.1 Anthony, James. *The Constitution Needs a Good Party: Good Government Comes from Good Boundaries.* Neuwoehner Press, 2018.

8.2 Anthony, James. "rConstitution Paper 3: Individual Rights Are Secured When Constitutional Powers Are Used." *rConstitution Papers: Offsetting Powers Secure Our Rights,* Neuwoehner Press, 2020, pp. 3.1–15.

8.3 USA Constitution, art. V.

8.4 Wayne Crews, Clyde, Jr. *Ten Thousand Commandments: An Annual Snapshot of the Federal Regulatory State.* Competitive Enterprise Institute, 2017, p. 33.

8.5 Natelson, Robert G. "The General Welfare Clause and the Public Trust: An Essay in Original Understanding." *University of Kansas Law Review,* vol. 52, 2003, pp. 1–56.

8.6 Eastman, John C. "Restoring the 'General' to the General Welfare Clause." *Chapman Law Review,* vol. 4, no. 1, 2001, pp. 63–87.

8.7 USA Constitution, art. I, sec. 8, cl. 3.

8.8 Barnett, Randy E. "The Original Meaning of the Commerce Clause." *The University of Chicago Law Review,* vol. 68, no. 1, 2001, pp. 101–47.

8.9 USA Constitution, art. I, sec. 8, cl. 18.

8.10 Natelson, Robert G. "The Agency Law Origins of the Necessary and Proper Clause." *Case Western Reserve Law Review,* vol. 55, 2004, pp. 243–322.

8.11 Perkins, Edwin J. *The Economy of Colonial America.* 2nd ed., Columbia University Press, 1988, pp. 190, 205.

[9.1] Anthony, James. *The Constitution Needs a Good Party: Good Government Comes from Good Boundaries.* Neuwoehner Press, 2018.

[9.2] *The Bible.* CSB Study Bible, Holman Bible Publishers, 2017, Job 3:16.

[9.3] *The Bible.* CSB Study Bible, Holman Bible Publishers, 2017, Genesis 25:21–22.

[9.4] *The Bible.* CSB Study Bible, Holman Bible Publishers, 2017, Psalms 139:13.

[9.5] *The Bible.* CSB Study Bible, Holman Bible Publishers, 2017, Luke 1:36.

[9.6] *The Bible.* CSB Study Bible, Holman Bible Publishers, 2017, Luke 1:41.

[9.7] Olasky, Marvin N., and Susan Northway Olasky. "The Crossover in Newspaper Coverage of Abortion from Murder to Liberation." *The Journalism Quarterly,* vol. 63, no. 1, 1986, pp. 31–7.

[9.8] Condic, Maureen L. "Preimplantation Stages of Human Development: The Biological and Moral Status of Early Embryos." *Is This Cell a Human Being?,* edited by Antoine Suarez and Joachim Huarte, Springer, 2011, pp. 25–43.

[9.9] Kestelman, Philip, and James Trussell. "Efficacy of the Simultaneous Use of Condoms and Spermicides." *Family Planning Perspectives,* vol. 23, no. 5, 1991, pp. 226–32.

[9.10] Scherwitzl, E. Berglund, et al. "Perfect-Use and Typical-Use Pearl Index of a Contraceptive Mobile App." *Contraception,* vol. 96, no. 6, 2017, pp. 420–5.

References

9.11 Cunningham, F., et al. *Williams Obstetrics.* 24th ed., McGraw-Hill, 2014, Chapter 5.

9.12 Milsom, Ian, and Tjeerd Korver. "Ovulation Incidence with Oral Contraceptives: A Literature Review." *Journal of Family Planning and Reproductive Health Care,* vol. 34, no. 4, 2008, pp. 237–46.

9.13 Ahuja, Meenakshi, and Pramod Pujari. "Ultra-Low-Dose Oral Contraceptive Pill: A New Approach to a Conventional Requirement." *International Journal of Reproduction, Contraception, Obstetrics and Gynecology,* vol. 6, no. 2, 2017, pp. 364–70.

9.14 Elomaa, Kaisa. *The Risk of Escape Ovulation under Treatment with Low-Dose Combined Oral Contraceptives.* Dissertation, University of Helsinki, 2001.

9.15 Jensen, Jeffrey T., and Daniel R. Mishell, Jr. "Family Planning: Contraception, Sterilization, and Pregnancy Termination." *Comprehensive Gynecology,* 6th edition, Elsevier, 2014, pp. 215–72: p. 226.

9.16 Shaklee, Harriet, and Baruch Fischhoff. "The Psychology of Contraceptive Surprises: Cumulative Risk and Contraceptive Effectiveness." *Journal of Applied Social Psychology,* vol. 20, no. 5, 1990, pp. 385–403.

9.17 Zinaman, Michael J., et al. "Estimates of Human Fertility and Pregnancy Loss." *Fertility and Sterility,* vol. 65, no. 3, 1996, pp. 503–9.

9.18 Reyna, Valerie F., and Frank Farley. "Risk and Rationality in Adolescent Decision Making: Implications for Theory, Practice, and Public Policy."

Psychological Science in the Public Interest, vol. 7, no. 1, 2006, pp. 1–44.

[9.19] Lebel, Catherine, et al. "Microstructural Maturation of the Human Brain from Childhood to Adulthood." *Neuroimage,* vol. 40, no. 3, 2008, pp. 1044–55.

[9.20] Cunningham, F., et al. *Williams Obstetrics.* 24th ed., McGraw-Hill, 2014, pp. 363–76.

[9.21] Denny, Colleen C., et al. "Induction of Fetal Demise before Pregnancy Termination: Practices of Family Planning Providers." *Contraception,* vol. 92, no. 3, 2015, pp. 241–5.

[9.22] Seth, Anil K. "Interoceptive Inference, Emotion, and the Embodied Self." *Trends in Cognitive Sciences,* vol. 17, no. 11, 2013, pp. 565–73.

[9.23] Xu, Xiaohe, et al. "The Timing of First Marriage: Are There Religious Variations?" *Journal of Family Issues,* vol. 26, no. 5, 2005, pp. 584–618.

[9.24] Uecker, Jeremy E., et al. "Losing My Religion: The Social Sources of Religious Decline in Early Adulthood." *Social Forces,* vol. 85, no. 4, 2007, pp. 1667–92.

[9.25] Hammond, Judith A., et al. "Religious Heritage and Teenage Marriage." *Review of Religious Research,* vol. 35, no. 2, 1993, pp. 117–33.

[9.26] *Unintended Pregnancy in the United States.* Guttmacher, 2016.

[9.27] "How Many Minutes of Commercials Are Shown in an Average TV Hour? The Number Has Been Steadily Climbing." *TVWeek,* 13 May 2014, www.tvweek.com/

tvbizwire/2014/05/how-many-minutes-of-commercial/. Accessed 18 Nov. 2017.

[9.28] Koloze, Jeff J. "Cinematic Treatment of Abortion: Alfie (1965) and The Cider House Rules (1999)." *LifeIssues.net*, 2006, www.lifeissues.net/writers/kol/kol_21cinematic1.html. Accessed 18 Nov. 2017.

[9.29] Gold, Judy, et al. *How to Talk about Abortion: A Guide to Rights-Based Messaging.* International Planned Parenthood Federation, 2015.

[9.30] Stulberg, Debra B., et al. "Abortion Provision among Practicing Obstetrician–Gynecologists." *Obstetrics and Gynecology*, vol. 118, no. 3, 2011, pp. 609–14.

[9.31] Curlin, Farr A., et al. "Religion, Conscience, and Controversial Clinical Practices." *New England Journal of Medicine*, vol. 356, no. 6, 2007, pp. 593–600.

[9.32] Joffe, Carole E., et al. "Uneasy Allies: Pro-Choice Physicians, Feminist Health Activists and the Struggle for Abortion Rights." *Sociology of Health & Illness*, vol. 26, no. 6, 2004, pp. 775–96.

[9.33] Halfmann, Drew. "Historical Priorities and the Responses of Doctors' Associations to Abortion Reform Proposals in Britain and the United States, 1960–1973." *Social Problems*, vol. 50, no. 4, 2003, pp. 567–91.

[9.34] USA Declaration of Independence, 1776.

[9.35] Lindert, Peter H., and Jeffrey G. Williamson. *Unequal Gains: American Growth and Inequality since 1700.* EPUB version, Princeton University Press, 2016, pp. 107–8.

9.36 Olson, Lester C. "Benjamin Franklin's Pictorial Representations of the British Colonies in America: A Study in Rhetorical Iconology." *Quarterly Journal of Speech,* vol. 73, no. 1, 1987, pp. 18–42.

9.37 USA Constitution, art. VI, cl. 2.

9.38 USA Constitution, amend. 5.

9.39 USA Constitution, art. II, sec. 1, cl. 8.

9.40 USA Constitution, art. VI, cl. 3.

9.41 Lindert, Peter H., and Jeffrey G. Williamson. *Unequal Gains: American Growth and Inequality since 1700.* EPUB version, Princeton University Press, 2016, pp. 61, 158.

9.42 USA Constitution, amend. 14, sec. 1.

9.43 Skowronek, Stephen, et al, editors. *The Progressives' Century: Political Reform, Constitutional Government, and the Modern American State.* Yale University Press, 2016.

9.44 "Conservative Review—Scorecard." *Conservative Review.com,* www.conservativereview.com/scorecard. Accessed 29 Jan. 2017.

9.45 "List of United States Presidential Elections by Electoral College Margin." *Wikipedia,* 13 June 2017, en.wikipedia.org/wiki/List_of_United_States_presidential_elections_by_Electoral_College_margin. Accessed 28 June 2017.

9.46 Rogers Hummel, Jeffrey. *Emancipating Slaves, Enslaving Free Men: A History of the American Civil War.* 2nd ed., Open Court, 2014.

References

9.47 Havrylyshyn, Oleh, et al. *25 Years of Reforms in Ex-Communist Countries: Fast and Extensive Reforms Led to Higher Growth and More Political Freedom.* Policy Analysis no. 795, Cato Institute, 12 July 2016.

10.1 Anthony, James. *The Constitution Needs a Good Party: Good Government Comes from Good Boundaries.* Neuwoehner Press, 2018.

10.2 Rogers Hummel, Jeffrey. "Martin Van Buren: The Greatest American President." *The Independent Review*, vol. 4, no. 2, 1999, pp. 255–81.

10.3 Wallis, John Joseph. "What Caused the Crisis of 1839?" *NBER Working Papers Series on Historical Factors in Long Run Growth*, no. 133, 2001.

10.4 Rothbard, Murray Newton. *A History of Money and Banking in the United States: The Colonial Era to World War II.* Ludwig von Mises Institute, 2002, pp. 90–104.

10.5 Smith, Walter Buckingham, and Arthur Harrison Cole. *Fluctuations in American Business, 1790–1860.* Harvard University Press, 1935, p. 158.

10.6 Rothbard, Murray Newton. *A History of Money and Banking in the United States: The Colonial Era to World War II.* Ludwig von Mises Institute, 2002, p. 103.

10.7 Rothbard, Murray Newton. *A History of Money and Banking in the United States: The Colonial Era to World War II.* Ludwig von Mises Institute, 2002, p. 91.

10.8 Sornette, Didier, and Ryan Woodard. "Financial Bubbles, Real Estate Bubbles, Derivative Bubbles, and the Financial and Economic Crisis." *Econophysics Approaches to Large-Scale Business Data and Financial Crisis,* Springer, 2010, pp. 101–48.

10.9 Salerno, Joseph T. "A Reformulation of Austrian Business Cycle Theory in Light of the Financial Crisis."

Quarterly Journal of Austrian Economics, vol. 15, no. 1, 2012, pp. 3–44.

[10.10] USA Constitution, amend. 5.

[10.11] USA Constitution, amend. 14, sec. 1.

[10.12] Bagus, Philipp, et al. "The Hubris of Hybrids." *Journal of Business Ethics*, vol. 145, no. 2, 2017, pp. 373–82.

[10.13] USA Constitution, art. I, sec. 8, cl. 1.

[10.14] USA Constitution, art. I, sec. 8, cl. 5.

[10.15] USA Constitution, art. I, sec. 8, cl. 18.

[10.16] USA Constitution, art. I, sec. 10, cl. 1.

[10.17] USA Constitution, amend. 10.

[10.18] McClanahan, Brion. *The Founding Fathers' Guide to the Constitution*. EPUB version, Regnery History, 2012, p. 61.

[10.19] Rothbard, Murray Newton. *A History of Money and Banking in the United States: The Colonial Era to World War II*. Ludwig von Mises Institute, 2002, pp. 65–8, 104–11.

[10.20] Hülsmann, Jörg Guido. "Legal Tender Laws and Fractional-Reserve Banking." *Journal of Libertarian Studies*, vol. 18, no. 3, 2004, pp. 33–55.

[10.21] Hazlitt, Henry. *Economics in One Lesson: The Shortest and Surest Way to Understand Basic Economics*. Revised and updated ed., Arlington House, 1979.

[10.22] Bonneau, Joseph, and Steven Goldfeder. "Five Myths about Bitcoin." *Washington Post*, 15 Dec. 2017.

10.23 Siegel, Jeremy J. *Stocks for the Long Run*. 2nd ed., McGraw-Hill, 1998, p. 4.

10.24 Siegel, Jeremy J. *Stocks for the Long Run*. 5th ed., McGraw-Hill Education, 2014, p. 6.

10.25 *Vanguard Total World Stock ETF Fact Sheet*. Vanguard, 20 Sep. 2017.

10.26 "Femto-." *Wikipedia*, 2 June 2018, en.wikipedia.org/wiki/Femto-. Accessed 24 Jan. 2019.

10.27 Iskyan, Kim. "China's Stock Markets Have Soared by 1,479% since 2003." *BusinessInsider.com*, 6 Nov. 2016, www.businessinsider.com/world-stock-market-capitalizations-2016-11. Accessed 27 Dec. 2017.

10.28 Koch, Charles G. *Good Profit: How Creating Value for Others Built One of the World's Most Successful Companies*. Crown Business, 2015.

10.29 Field, Alexander J. *A Great Leap Forward: 1930s Depression and US Economic Growth*. Yale University Press, 2011.

10.30 Simon, Julian L. "More People, Greater Wealth, More Resources, Healthier Environment." *Economic Affairs*, vol. 14, no. 3, Apr. 1994, pp. 22–9.

References

11.1 Anthony, James. *The Constitution Needs a Good Party: Good Government Comes from Good Boundaries.* Neuwoehner Press, 2018.

11.2 Harrison, Mark. "The Economics of World War II: An Overview." *The Economics of World War II: Six Great Powers in International Comparison*, edited by Mark Harrison, Cambridge University Press, 2000, pp. 1–42.

11.3 McBride, William. "What Is the Evidence on Taxes and Growth?" *Tax Foundation Special Report*, no. 207, 2012.

11.4 Reynolds, Alan. "Big Government, Big Recession." *The Wall Street Journal*, vol. 254, no. 44, 21 Aug. 2009, p. A13.

11.5 Higgs, Robert. *Depression, War, and Cold War: Studies in Political Economy.* Oxford University Press, 2006, pp. 61–80.

11.6 Pryce-Jones, David. *The Strange Death of the Soviet Empire.* Metropolitan Books, 1995.

11.7 Harrison, Mark. "The Economics of World War II: An Overview." *The Economics of World War II: Six Great Powers in International Comparison*, edited by Mark Harrison, Cambridge University Press, 2000, pp. 1–42; p. 10.

11.8 Higgs, Robert. *Depression, War, and Cold War: Studies in Political Economy.* Oxford University Press, 2006, p. 106.

11.9 Higgs, Robert. *Neither Liberty nor Safety: Fear, Ideology, and the Growth of Government.* Independent Institute, 2007, pp. 101–23.

11.10 Geisst, Charles R. *Collateral Damaged: The Marketing of Consumer Debt to America.* Bloomberg Press, 2009, p. 56.

11.11 Bierman, Harold. *Beating the Bear: Lessons from the 1929 Crash Applied to Today's World.* Praeger, 2010, pp. 156–61.

11.12 Powell, Jim. *FDR's Folly: How Roosevelt and His New Deal Prolonged the Great Depression.* Crown Forum, 2003.

11.13 Rogers Hummel, Jeffrey. "Martin Van Buren: The Greatest American President." *The Independent Review,* vol. 4, no. 2, 1999, pp. 255–81.

11.14 Rothbard, Murray Newton. *A History of Money and Banking in the United States: The Colonial Era to World War II.* Ludwig von Mises Institute, 2002, p. 103.

11.15 Higgs, Robert. *Depression, War, and Cold War: Studies in Political Economy.* Oxford University Press, 2006, pp. 3–29.

11.16 "Serenity Prayer." *Wikipedia,* 11 Jan. 2018, en.wikipedia.org/wiki/Serenity_Prayer. Accessed 16 Jan. 2018.

11.17 Rummel, Rudolph J. *Lethal Politics: Soviet Genocide and Mass Murder since 1917.* Routledge, 2017, p. 10.

11.18 Yakovlev, Aleksandr Nikolaevich. *A Century of Violence in Soviet Russia.* Yale University Press, 2002, p. 237.

[11.19] Rummel, Rudolph J. *Never Again: Ending War, Democide, & Famine Through Democratic Freedom.* Llumina Press, 2005, pp. 224, 193.

[11.20] USA Constitution, amend. 10.

[11.21] USA Constitution, art. I, sec. 1.

[11.22] USA Constitution, art. I, sec. 8, cl. 1.

[11.23] USA Constitution, art. I, sec. 8, cl. 2.

[11.24] USA Constitution, art. I, sec. 8, cl. 13.

[11.25] USA Constitution, art. I, sec. 8, cl. 17.

[11.26] USA Constitution, art. I, sec. 8, cl. 12.

[11.27] USA Constitution, art. I, sec. 8, cl. 15.

[11.28] USA Constitution, art. I, sec. 8, cl. 16.

[11.29] USA Constitution, art. I, sec. 8, cl. 10.

[11.30] USA Constitution, art. I, sec. 8, cl. 11.

[11.31] USA Constitution, art. I, sec. 8, cl. 14.

[11.32] Kilner, Peter. "Military Leaders' Obligation to Justify Killing in War." *Military Review,* vol. 82, no. 2, Mar.–Apr. 2002, pp. 24–31.

[11.33] Garvin, David A. *Learning in Action: A Guide to Putting the Learning Organization to Work.* Harvard Business School Press, 2000, pp. 106–16.

[11.34] *Process Safety Leading and Lagging Metrics ... You Don't Improve What You Don't Measure.* Center for Chemical Process Safety, 2007, pp. 35–8.

[11.35] McKinnon, Ron C. *Safety Management: Near Miss Identification, Recognition, and Investigation.* CRC Press, 2012, pp. 97–109.

[11.36] Parks, W. Hays. "Deadly Force Is Authorized." *US Naval Institute Proceedings,* vol. 127, no. 1., Jan. 2001, pp. 32–7.

[11.37] Dekker, Sidney. *Just Culture: Balancing Safety and Accountability.* Ashgate, 2007.

[11.38] Mathews, Mitford M., editor. *A Dictionary of Americanisms on Historical Principles.* Vol. I, University of Chicago Press, 1951, pp. 198–9.

[11.39] Etzioni, Amitai. "Rules of Engagement and Abusive Citizens." *PRISM,* vol. 4, no. 4, Apr. 2014, pp. 87–102.

[11.40] USA Constitution, amend. 5.

[11.41] Cooperstein, Theodore M. "Letters of Marque and Reprisal: The Constitutional Law and Practice of Privateering." *Journal of Maritime Law & Commerce,* vol. 40, no. 2, 2009, pp. 221–59.

References

[12.1] Anthony, James. *The Constitution Needs a Good Party: Good Government Comes from Good Boundaries.* Neuwoehner Press, 2018.

[12.2] United States, Advisory Commission on Intergovernmental Relations. *Categorical Grants: Their Role and Design.* Government Printing Office, 1978, p. 5.

[12.3] Dilger, Robert Jay, and Eugene Boyd. *Block Grants: Perspectives and Controversies.* Congressional Research Service, 2014, p. 3.

[12.4] Dilger, Robert Jay, and Eugene Boyd. *Block Grants: Perspectives and Controversies.* Congressional Research Service, 2014, p. 6.

[12.5] Dilger, Robert Jay. *Federal Grants to State and Local Governments: A Historical Perspective on Contemporary Issues.* Congressional Research Service, 2017, p. 5.

[12.6] Edwards, Chris. "Federal Aid to the States: Historical Cause of Government Growth and Bureaucracy." *Policy Analysis*, no. 593, 2007, pp. 14–5.

[12.7] Edwards, Chris. "Federal Aid to the States: Historical Cause of Government Growth and Bureaucracy." *Policy Analysis*, no. 593, 2007, pp. 12–3.

[12.8] Anthony, James. "rConstitution Paper 8: Laws That Exceed Enumerated Powers Are Unconstitutional." *rConstitution Papers: Offsetting Powers Secure Our Rights,* Neuwoehner Press, 2020, pp. 8.1–8.

[12.9] Åström, Karl Johan, and Tore Hägglund. *Advanced PID Control.* ISA, 2006, p. 26.

12.10 Ziegler, J. G., and N. B. Nichols. "Process Lags in Automatic-Control Circuits." *Transactions of the A.S.M.E.*, vol. 65, no. 5, 1943, pp. 433–44.

12.11 Bars, R., et al. "Control Systems—Cascade Loops." *Process Control and Optimization*, edited by Bela G. Liptak, 4th ed., CRC Press, 2006, pp. 148–56.

12.12 Edwards, James Rolph. "The Costs of Public Income Redistribution and Private Charity." *Journal of Libertarian Studies*, vol. 21, no. 2, 2007, pp. 3–20.

12.13 Payne, James L. "Government Fails, Long Live Government! The Rise of 'Failurism.'" *The Independent Review*, vol. 21, no. 1, 2016, pp. 121–32.

12.14 Dahlgren, Eric, et al. "Small Modular Infrastructure." *The Engineering Economist*, vol. 58, no. 4, 2013, pp. 231–64.

12.15 Merrow, E. W. *An Analysis of Cost Improvement in Chemical Process Technologies.* Rand, 1989.

12.16 Blackburn, Joseph D., Gary D. Scudder, and Luk N. Van Wassenhove. "Improving Speed and Productivity of Software Development: A Global Survey of Software Developers." *IEEE Transactions on Software Engineering*, vol. 22, no. 12, 1996, pp. 875–85.

12.17 Brooks, Frederick P., Jr. *The Mythical Man-Month: Essays on Software Engineering.* 20th anniversary ed., Addison Wesley Longman, 1995.

12.18 Baumann, Hans D. *Building Lean Companies: How to Keep Companies Profitable as They Grow.* Morgan James Publishing, 2009, p. 17.

References

[13.1] Anthony, James. *The Constitution Needs a Good Party: Good Government Comes from Good Boundaries.* Neuwoehner Press, 2018.

[13.2] USA Constitution, art. I, sec. 3, cl. 1.

[13.3] USA Constitution, amend. 17.

[13.4] USA Constitution, art. I, sec. 3, cl. 4.

[13.5] USA Constitution, art. I, sec. 7, cl. 2.

[13.6] USA Constitution, art. VI.

[13.7] USA Constitution, art. I, sec. 5, cl. 2.

[13.8] Havrylyshyn, Oleh, et al. *25 Years of Reforms in Ex-Communist Countries: Fast and Extensive Reforms Led to Higher Growth and More Political Freedom.* Policy Analysis no. 795, Cato Institute, 12 July 2016.

[13.9] "Forecasts, Macro Data, Transition Indicators." *European Bank for Reconstruction and Development,* www.ebrd.com/what-we-do/economic-research-and-data/data/forecasts-macro-data-transition-indicators.html. Accessed 18 Oct. 2017.

[13.10] Anthony, James. "rConstitution Paper 5: Laws That Direct the Executive or Direct the Judiciary Are Unconstitutional." *rConstitution Papers: Offsetting Powers Secure Our Rights,* Neuwoehner Press, 2020, pp. 9.1–30.

[13.11] Skowronek, Stephen, et al, editors. *The Progressives' Century: Political Reform, Constitutional Government, and the Modern American State.* Yale University Press, 2016.

14.1 Anthony, James. *The Constitution Needs a Good Party: Good Government Comes from Good Boundaries.* Neuwoehner Press, 2018.

14.2 USA Constitution, art. I, sec. 10, cl. 3.

14.3 USA Constitution, art. I, sec. 10, cl. 1.

14.4 Weinfeld, Abraham C. "What Did the Framers of the Federal Constitution Mean by 'Agreements or Compacts'?" *The University of Chicago Law Review,* vol. 3, no. 3, 1936, pp. 453–64.

14.5 USA Constitution, amend. 10.

14.6 USA Constitution, art. VI, cl. 2

14.7 USA Constitution, art. I, sec. 8, cl. 1.

14.8 USA Constitution, art. II, sec. 3.

14.9 Anthony, James. "rConstitution Paper 8: Laws That Exceed Enumerated Powers Are Unconstitutional." *rConstitution Papers: Offsetting Powers Secure Our Rights,* Neuwoehner Press, 2020, pp. 8.1–8.

14.10 USA Constitution, art. II, sec. 2, cl. 2.

14.11 Bestor, Arthur. "Respective Roles of Senate and President in the Making and Abrogation of Treaties—The Original Intent of the Framers of the Constitution Historically Examined." *Washington Law Review,* vol. 55, 1979, pp. 1–135.

14.12 McGee, Robert W. "The Fatal Flaw in NAFTA, GATT and All Other Trade Agreements." *Northwestern Journal of International Law & Business,* vol. 14, no. 3, 1994, pp. 549–65.

References

14.13 USA Constitution, art. I, sec. 7, cl. 2.

14.14 Anthony, James. "rConstitution Paper 13: Filibuster/Cloture Is Unconstitutional." *rConstitution Papers: Offsetting Powers Secure Our Rights*, Neuwoehner Press, 2020, pp. 13.1–9.

14.15 "Conservative Review—Scorecard." *Conservative Review.com*, www.conservativereview.com/scorecard. Accessed 8 May 2018.

R14.2

15.1 Anthony, James. *The Constitution Needs a Good Party: Good Government Comes from Good Boundaries.* Neuwoehner Press, 2018.

15.2 Dudley, Leonard, and Claude Montmarquette. "The Demand for Military Expenditures: An International Comparison." *Public Choice,* vol. 37, no. 1, 1981, pp. 5–31.

15.3 Olson, Mancur, and Richard Zeckhauser. "An Economic Theory of Alliances." *The Review of Economics and Statistics,* vol. 48, no. 3, 1966, pp. 266–79.

15.4 Cornes, Richard, and Todd Sandler. *The Theory of Externalities, Public Goods, and Club Goods.* 2nd ed., Cambridge University Press, 1996.

15.5 Kertzer, Joshua D., and Thomas Zeitzoff. "A Bottom-Up Theory of Public Opinion about Foreign Policy." *American Journal of Political Science,* vol. 61, no. 3, 2017, pp. 543–58.

15.6 Tago, Atsushi. "When Are Democratic Friends Unreliable? The Unilateral Withdrawal of Troops from the 'Coalition of the Willing'." *Journal of Peace Research,* vol. 46, no. 2, 2009, pp. 219–34.

15.7 Kreps, Sarah. "Elite Consensus as a Determinant of Alliance Cohesion: Why Public Opinion Hardly Matters for NATO-Led Operations in Afghanistan." *Foreign Policy Analysis,* vol. 6, no. 3, 2010, pp. 191–215.

15.8 "War in Afghanistan (2001–present)." *Wikipedia,* 5 June 2018, en.wikipedia.org/wiki/War_in_Afghanistan_(2001%E2%80%93present). Accessed 6 June 2018.

References

[15.9] Carpenter, Daniel. *Reputation and Power: Organizational Image and Pharmaceutical Regulation at the FDA*. Princeton University Press, 2014.

16.1 Anthony, James. *The Constitution Needs a Good Party: Good Government Comes from Good Boundaries.* Neuwoehner Press, 2018.

16.2 Barnett, Randy E. *Our Republican Constitution: Securing the Liberty and Sovereignty of We the People.* Broadside Books, 2016, pp. 167–8.

16.3 Anthony, James. "rConstitution Paper 3: Individual Rights Are Secured When Constitutional Powers Are Used." *rConstitution Papers: Offsetting Powers Secure Our Rights,* Neuwoehner Press, 2020, pp. 3.1–15.

16.4 Anthony, James. "rConstitution Paper 13: Filibuster/Cloture Is Unconstitutional." *rConstitution Papers: Offsetting Powers Secure Our Rights,* Neuwoehner Press, 2020, pp. 13.1–9.

16.5 USA Constitution, art. II, sec. 4.

16.6 USA Constitution, art. VI, cl. 3.

16.7 Melton, Buckner F., Jr. "Let Me Be Blunt: In Blount, the Senate Never Said that Senators Aren't Impeachable." *Quinnipiac Law Review,* vol. 33, 2014, pp. 33–57.

16.8 Cole, Jared P., and Todd Garvey. *Impeachment and Removal.* Congressional Research Service, 2015.

16.9 USA Constitution, art. II, sec. 4.

16.10 McGinnis, John O. "Impeachment: The Structural Understanding." *The George Washington Law Review,* vol. 67, no. 3, 1999, pp. 650–65.

16.11 USA Constitution, art. I, sec. 3, cl. 7.

16.12 USA Constitution, art. II, sec. 2, cl. 1.

References

16.13 Verkerke, J. Hoult. "An Empirical Perspective on Indefinite Term Employment Contracts: Resolving the Just Cause Debate." *Wisconsin Law Review*, 1995, pp. 837–917.

16.14 Epstein, Richard A. "In Defense of the Contract at Will." *The University of Chicago Law Review*, vol. 51, no. 4, 1984, pp. 947–82.

16.15 Kalt, Brian C. "The Constitutional Case for the Impeachability of Former Federal Officials: An Analysis of the Law, History, and Practice of Late Impeachment." *Texas Review of Law & Politics*, vol. 6, no. 1, 2001, pp. 13–135.

16.16 USA Constitution, art. I, sec. 2, cl. 5.

16.17 USA Constitution, art. I, sec. 3, cl. 6.

16.18 Black, Charles L., Jr. *Impeachment: A Handbook.* Yale University Press, 1974.

16.19 USA Constitution, art. VI, cl. 2.

16.20 Roots, Roger. "If It's Not a Runaway, It's Not a Real Grand Jury." *Creighton Law Review*, vol. 33, no. 4, 2000, pp. 821–42.

16.21 Turley, Jonathan. "Congress as Grand Jury: The Role of the House of Representatives in the Impeachment of an American President." *The George Washington Law Review*, vol. 67, no. 3, 1999, pp. 735–90.

16.22 McGinnis, John O., and Michael B. Rappaport. "Our Supermajoritarian Constitution." *Texas Law Review*, vol. 80, no. 4, 2001, pp. 703–806.

16.23 Perkins, Edwin J. *The Economy of Colonial America*. 2nd ed., Columbia University Press, 1988, pp. 190, 205.

16.24 "Conservative Review—Scorecard." *Conservative Review.com*, www.conservativereview.com/scorecard. Accessed 8 May 2018.

References

17.1 Simon, Julian L. "More People, Greater Wealth, More Resources, Healthier Environment." *Economic Affairs,* vol. 14, no. 3, Apr. 1994, pp. 22–9.

17.2 Skowronek, Stephen, et al, editors. *The Progressives' Century: Political Reform, Constitutional Government, and the Modern American State.* Yale University Press, 2016.

17.3 Hamburger, Philip. *The Administrative Threat.* Encounter Books, 2017.

17.4 USA Constitution, art. I, sec. 1.

17.5 Anthony, James. "rConstitution Paper 4: Laws That Aren't Readable Aren't Constitutional." *rConstitution Papers: Offsetting Powers Secure Our Rights,* Neuwoehner Press, 2020, pp. 4.1–14.

17.6 Anthony, James. "rConstitution Paper 6: Laws That Delegate Legislative Authority Are Unconstitutional." *rConstitution Papers: Offsetting Powers Secure Our Rights,* Neuwoehner Press, 2020, pp. 6.1–10.

17.7 USA Constitution, art. II, sec. 1, cl. 1.

17.8 Anthony, James. "rConstitution Paper 5: Laws That Direct the Executive or Direct the Judiciary Are Unconstitutional." *rConstitution Papers: Offsetting Powers Secure Our Rights,* Neuwoehner Press, 2020, pp. 5.1–9.

17.9 Anthony, James. "rConstitution Paper 3: Individual Rights Are Secured When Constitutional Powers Are Used." *rConstitution Papers: Offsetting Powers Secure Our Rights,* Neuwoehner Press, 2020, pp. 3.1–15.

17.10 USA Constitution, art. III.

[17.11] USA Constitution, amend. 10.

[17.12] Natelson, Robert G. "The Enumerated Powers of States." *Nevada Law Journal,* vol. 3, 2003, pp. 469–94.

[17.13] USA Constitution, art. VI, cl. 3.

[17.14] USA Constitution, art. II, sec. 1, cl. 8.

[17.15] USA Constitution, art. I, sec. 5, cl. 2.

[17.16] Verkerke, J. Hoult. "An Empirical Perspective on Indefinite Term Employment Contracts: Resolving the Just Cause Debate." *Wisconsin Law Review,* 1995, pp. 837–917.

[17.17] USA Constitution, art. I, sec. 3, cl. 7.

[17.18] USA Constitution, art. I, sec. 2, cl. 5.

[17.19] USA Constitution, art. I, sec. 3, cl. 6.

[17.20] Anthony, James. "rConstitution Paper 16: Failure to Impeach and Convict Denies People Their Rights." *rConstitution Papers: Offsetting Powers Secure Our Rights,* Neuwoehner Press, 2020, pp. 16.1–24.

[17.21] Anthony, James. *The Constitution Needs a Good Party: Good Government Comes from Good Boundaries.* Neuwoehner Press, 2018.

References

18.1 Anthony, James. "rConstitution Paper 3: Individual Rights Are Secured When Constitutional Powers Are Used." *rConstitution Papers: Offsetting Powers Secure Our Rights*, Neuwoehner Press, 2020, pp. 3.1–15

18.2 Rothbard, Murray N. *The Progressive Era*. Edited by Patrick Newman, Mises Institute, 2017, p. 111.

18.3 Martis, Kenneth C., et al. *The Historical Atlas of Political Parties in the United States Congress, 1789–1989*. Macmillan Publishing Company, 1989.

18.4 Martin, Margaret C. *The First Test: Madison's Strategy, the Constitution, and the War of 1812*. MS thesis, Air University, 2010.

18.5 Miller, Nathan. *The US Navy: A History*. 3rd ed., Naval Institute Press, 1997. EPUB version, 2014, p. 99.

18.6 Elsea, Jennifer K., and Matthew C. Weed. *Declarations of War and Authorizations for the Use of Military Force: Historical Background and Legal Implications*. Congressional Research Service, 2014, p. 81.

18.7 Rothbard, Murray Newton. *A History of Money and Banking in the United States: The Colonial Era to World War II*. Ludwig von Mises Institute, 2002, pp. 68–80.

18.8 Whaples, Robert. "Were Andrew Jackson's Policies 'Good for the Economy'?" *The Independent Review*, vol. 18, no. 4, 2014, pp. 545–58.

18.9 Jackson, Andrew. "First Inaugural Address." *A Compilation of the Messages and Papers of the Presidents, 1789–1897*, edited by James Daniel Richardson, vol. 2, Washington, D.C., 1897, pp. 436–8.

18.10 Race, Charles. "The Rise of the American Navy 1775–1914." *HistoryNet.com*, 7 Sep. 2016, www.historynet.com/the-rise-of-the-american-navy-1775-1914.htm. Accessed 10 Sep. 2018.

18.11 Cole, Donald B. *The Presidency of Andrew Jackson*. University Press of Kansas, 1993, p. 134.

18.12 Rogers Hummel, Jeffrey. "Martin Van Buren: The Greatest American President." *The Independent Review*, vol. 4, no. 2, 1999, pp. 255–81.

18.13 Rothbard, Murray Newton. *A History of Money and Banking in the United States: The Colonial Era to World War II*. Ludwig von Mises Institute, 2002, pp. 82–122.

18.14 Lane, Carl. "The Elimination of the National Debt in 1835 and the Meaning of Jacksonian Democracy." *Essays in Economic & Business History*, vol. 25, 2007, pp. 67–78.

18.15 Schweikart, Larry. "Jacksonian Ideology, Currency Control and Central Banking: A Reappraisal." *The Historian*, vol. 51, no. 1, 1988, pp. 78–102.

18.16 Burnham, Walter Dean, et al. "Partisan Realignment: A Systemic Perspective." *The History of American Electoral Behavior*, edited by Joel H. Silbey and Allan G. Bogue, Princeton University Press, 1978, pp. 45–94; p. 65.

18.17 Gienapp, William E. *The Origins of the Republican Party, 1852–1856*. Oxford University Press, 1987, pp. 4, 443–8.

18.18 Friedman, Milton, and Anna Schwartz. *A Monetary History of the United States, 1867–1960*. Princeton University Press, 1963. EPUB version, 2008, p. 221.

References

18.19 Rothbard, Murray N. *The Progressive Era*. Edited by Patrick Newman, Mises Institute, 2017, pp. 163–97.

18.20 Peters, Gerhard. "Voter Turnout in Presidential Elections: 1828–2012." *The American Presidency Project*, Gerhard Peters and John T. Wooley, 2018, www.presidency.ucsb.edu/data/turnout.php. Accessed 12 Sep. 2018.

18.21 Higgs, Robert. *Crisis and Leviathan: Critical Episodes in the Growth of American Government*. Oxford University Press, 1987.

18.22 Anthony, James. "rConstitution Paper 11: Laws Authorizing Military Action Are Unconstitutional." *rConstitution Papers: Offsetting Powers Secure Our Rights*, Neuwoehner Press, 2020, pp. 11.1–24.

18.23 USA Constitution, art. I, sec. 10, cl. 1.

18.24 Parks, Larry. "Six Reasons Why Promoting the Gold Standard Is a Mistake." *FAME.org*, 4 June 2015, fame.org/six-reasons-why-promoting-the-gold-standard-is-a-mistake. Accessed 24 Sep. 2018.

18.25 Anthony, James. "rConstitution Paper 10: Fractional-Reserve Banking Is Unconstitutional." *rConstitution Papers: Offsetting Powers Secure Our Rights*, Neuwoehner Press, 2020, pp. 10.1–30.

18.26 USA Constitution, amend. 5.

18.27 USA Constitution, amend. 14, sec. 1.

18.28 Khan, Ali. "The Evolution of Money: A Story of Constitutional Nullification." *University of Cincinnati Law Review*, vol. 67, 1999, pp. 393–443.

[18.29] North, Gary. "How to End the Fed, and How Not To." *Mises.org*, 10 Sep. 2012, mises.org/print/4510. Accessed 22 Sep. 2018.

[18.30] Wallison, Peter J. *Dissent from the Majority Report of the Financial Crisis Inquiry Commission*. American Enterprise Institute for Public Policy Research, 2011, pp. 2–3.

[18.31] USA Constitution, art. II, sec. 1, cl. 8.

[18.32] Bagus, Philipp, et al. "On the Necessary and Sufficient Conditions for Legitimate Banking Contracts." *Journal of Business Ethics*, vol. 147, no. 3, 2018, pp. 669–78.

[18.33] Horowitz, Daniel. "20 Ideas to Crush Obamacare and Cure America's Health Care Crisis." *Conservative Review.com*, 8 Mar. 2017, www.conservativereview.com/news/20-ideas-to-crush-obamacare-and-cure-americas-health-care-crisis/. Accessed 25 Sep. 2018.

[18.34] Piñera, José. "The Success of Chile's Privatized Social Security." *Cato Policy Report*, vol. 18, no. 4, July/Aug. 1995, pp. 1, 10–1.

[18.35] Anthony, James. *The Constitution Needs a Good Party: Good Government Comes from Good Boundaries*. Neuwoehner Press, 2018.

[18.36] Anthony, James. "rConstitution Paper 2: Washington, Reagan, and Everyone Else." *rConstitution Papers: Offsetting Powers Secure Our Rights*, Neuwoehner Press, 2020, pp. 2.1–10.

Index

A
abortion
  choices and, 9.8–9.14
  evidence that unborn
    babies are alive,
    9.2–9.4
  government people
    ignoring Constitution,
    Declaration, 9.1–9.2
  impeachment and,
    16.20–16.21
  return to constitutional
    protection of life,
    9.25–9.30
  simultaneous
    contraception for
    preventing pregnancy,
    9.4–9.7, 9.30
agency people
  congressional oversight
    of, 17.6–17.15
  judicial powers
    unconstitutionally
    granted to, 5.8
  legislative powers
    unconstitutionally
    granted to, 6.5–6.10
  misconduct and,
    16.19–16.20,
    16.21–16.22
  not entitled to jobs,
    16.11–16.12
  Progressives and, 17.8,
    17.15–17.17
  terms of employment
    governed by
    Constitution,
    17.13–17.14
  unconstitutional coercion
    and, 17.8
  unreadable laws and,
    4.1–4.2, 4.4, 4.11
American Medical
  Association, early position
  on abortion, 9.13
Articles of Confederation, 8.7
at-will employment, 16.11–
  16.12, 16.15, 17.14
Austrian economics,
  10.5–10.10

B
Baldwin, Tammy, 14.18, 16.19
Barnett, Randy, 18.14

I.1

Benton, Thomas Hart, 18.3
Bill of Rights, 5.7
block grants
   as big government, 12.1–12.3
   coercion by national government people and, 12.13–12.14
   detrimental character of government spending and, 12.4–12.6
   free cooperation and, 12.6–12.10
   minimal centralized government control and, 12.14–12.16
   state-government coercion and, 12.10–12.12
Blunt, Roy, 14.18
boundaries, good
   citizens empowered through knowledge and, 1.13–1.14
   Financial Crisis of 2007 and, 1.4–1.8, 1.11–1.13
   government scope and, 3.2–3.15
   importance of, 1.4–1.8, 17.6–17.7
   limiting government people, 1.2–1.4, 17.6–17.7
   limiting losses and, 16.4–16.6
   securing freedom, 1.8–1.11
   treaties as violations of, 14.6–14.7
Burr, Richard, 14.18
Bush, George H. W., 2.10
Bush, George W., 1.13

C

categorical-grant spending, 12.2–12.3
caucuses, state, new party design and, 18.17–18.18
central bank, USA, 10.1, 10.17–10.18
centralized government, voter rejection of, 2.9–2.10
change, fast, 12.4, 13.5–13.7
Civil War, USA, 9.19, 10.4, 14.16, 18.6
Clean Air Act (1970), 6.3–6.4
Cleveland, Grover, 18.6–18.7
Clinton, Hillary, 16.21–16.22
Commerce Clause, 8.6
common stocks, value of, 10.20–10.29
Community Reinvestment Act, 1.6
Congress. *see also* legislative branch
   agencies and, 17.8–17.11, 17.16
   block grants and, 12.1
   complying with the Constitution on abortion, 9.26–9.27
   congressional oversight. *see* separate entry
   expulsion of members, 17.13
   fractional-reserve banking and, 10.1, 10.18
   impeachment and, 16.22
   lawmaking power vested solely in, 17.8–17.9

Index

republican Constitution Party and, 18.17–18.18
terms of employment governed by Constitution, 17.13
treaties and, 14.1, 14.2, 14.9, 14.11, 14.13
warmaking powers of, 11.1, 11.14–11.16, 11.18–11.19, 11.21–11.24, 17.1–17.6
congressional oversight of agencies, 17.6–17.15
Progressives and, 17.15–17.17
of war, 17.1–17.6
constant money stock, 10.16–10.20
Constitution
agencies and, 17.6–17.17
Article I, 1.3, 1.11, 8.1–8.5, 18.15–18.19
Article I, Section 8, 1.11, 8.1–8.5
Article II, 1.3, 18.16
Article II, Section 1, 9.20
Article III, 1.3, 5.7, 5.9
Article IV, 18.16
Article V, 9.20, 18.16
Article VI, 9.20–9.21, 18.16
Article VII, 18.16
Bill of Rights, 5.7
block grants and, 12.1, 12.3, 12.15
boundaries limiting government people, 1.2–1.4, 1.8–1.12, 2.10, 3.1–3.15
Commerce Clause, 8.6
congressional oversight of presidents conducting war and, 17.1–17.6
constant money stock and, 10.16–10.20
creation of government agencies and, 17.8
enumerated powers, 8.1–8.8
enumerated powers in. *see* enumerated powers
failure to use constitutional powers to end slavery, 9.16–9.19, 9.21
failure to impeach and, 16.1–16.2
forward basing and, 15.4–15.6
Fourteenth Amendment, 9.19, 9.20
fractional reserve banking and, 10.1, 10.16–10.19, 10.29
freedom to shop and work, 17.7–17.8
General Welfare Clause, 8.5–8.6
George Washington and, 2.4–2.6
government brought into alignment with, 18.10–18.14
government people ignoring right to life, 9.1–9.2
government scope and, 3.1–3.15
impeachment and, 16.1–16.4, 16.6–16.12, 16.14, 16.16–16.22, 16.24

I.3

laws directing executive branch, 5.3–5.6, 5.8–5.9
laws directing judicial branch, 5.6–5.9
legislative authority in, 6.1–6.10
lossy money stock, property rights, 10.29
misleading laws and, 7.1, 7.14
money and, 10.1, 10.16–10.19, 10.28–10.30, 18.11–18.14
moral war and, 15.1–15.4
Necessary and Proper Clause, 8.6
new party design and, 18.14–18.19
oath or affirmation to, 17.11–17.13
peacemaking boundaries in, 11.1, 11.14–11.24
rights protection for individual property in money, 10.17–10.18, 10.28–10.30
Ronald Reagan and, 2.7, 2.9
simple-majority voting and, 13.1–13.9
slavery and, 9.16–9.19, 9.21, 9.27–9.28
structural protections securing right to life, 9.19–9.30
structural protections securing rights, 9.14–9.16, 9.19–9.30, 13.8
terms of employment of government people and, 17.13–17.14
treaties and, 14.1–14.5, 14.13, 14.17–14.19
Constitutional Convention, 2.4, 5.4, 10.17
Consumer Financial Protection Bureau, 6.7
control interactions
 coercion by national government people and, 12.13–12.14
 coercion by state government people and, 12.10–12.12
 free cooperation and, 12.6–12.10
 minimal centralized government control and, 12.14–12.16
Cordray, Richard, 6.7
cryptocurrency, 10.19–10.20
customers, 7.12, 10.11, 10.26–10.28, 14.10–14.11
 adding value. *also see* customers, control by, *also see* shopping, adding value through, 7.2–7.6, 7.11, 16.2
 control by, 1.10, 5.4, 6.5, 12.5–12.10, 12.12–12.16

D

Declaration of Independence, 2.4, 2.6, 3.1–3.2, 9.14, 9.16, 10.1
Democratic Party, 10.2–10.4, 18.3–18.5, 18.6–18.8
Department of Housing and Urban Development, 1.6

Index

diethylene glycol, 7.8–7.9

E
Eban, Abba, 1.4
education, abortion and,
  9.11–9.12
Eisenhower, Dwight, 2.7
electoral vote, 2.1–2.2
enumerated powers. *see also*
  scope, government
  block grants and, 12.3,
    12.15
  judicial opinions outside,
    3.9
  laws that exceed,
    1.11, 4.12, 8.1–8.8,
    10.17–10.18, 17.11,
    18.10
  powers not prohibited to
    the states, 17.11
  securing individual
    rights, 9.14–9.15,
    9.17–9.18
  treaties and, 14.3
error cycles, government
  money, 10.5–10.10
Evans, Thomas, 2.7
executive branch
  agencies and, 17.9–17.10
  executive power vested
    in president, 13.7,
    17.9–17.10
  impeachment and, 16.17
  laws directing, 5.1–5.6,
    5.8–5.9
  offsetting powers and,
    16.6–16.9
  Progressive dominance
    and, 17.16
  scope of powers, 3.7,
    3.9–3.11, 3.14
  terms of employment
    governed by
    Constitution,
    17.13–17.14

F
FBI, misconduct by,
  16.21–16.22
FCIC, 18.13
FDIC, 18.13
Federal Home Loan
  Mortgage Corporation
  (FHLMC; "Freddie Mac"),
  1.5–1.6, 1.11–1.12, 18.13
Federal Housing
  Administration, 1.6
Federal National Mortgage
  Association (FNMA;
  "Fannie Mae"), 1.5–1.6,
  1.11–1.12, 18.13
Federal Reserve, ending,
  18.12–18.13
femtoshares, 10.25–10.29
Ferling, John, 2.3
filibuster/cloture, 13.1–13.9
financial crisis of 1837,
  10.2–10.5, 18.3–18.4
financial crisis of 1839,
  10.2–10.5, 18.3–18.4
financial crisis of 2007,
  1.4–1.8, 1.11–1.13
financial crisis prevention,
  18.10–18.14
financial cycles, government
  money error (GME;
  "Gimme") cycles,
  10.5–10.10
Food and Drug
  Administration (FDA),
  regulation of drugs by,
  7.6–7.12

I.5

formal adjudication, 6.6
forward basing, 15.4–15.6
formal rulemaking, 6.6
fractional-reserve banking
 first Republican Party
  and, 18.2
 government money error
  cycles and, 10.5–10.10
 government people
  defying Declaration,
  Constitution, 10.1
 lossy money stock and,
  10.10–10.16
 political parties and,
  18.9, 18.11
 productive money stock
  and, 10.20–10.30
 repeal of laws allowing,
  18.13
 Van Buren's "second
  declaration of
  independence" and,
  10.2–10.5
Franklin, Benjamin, 9.16
free cooperation, 12.6–12.10
French and Indian War, 2.3
FSLIC, 18.13

G
General Electric, unions and,
 2.7–2.8
General Welfare Clause,
 8.5–8.6
George III, King, 1.2
gold, value of, 10.21
gold or silver backed
 currency, 10.1–10.2, 10.12,
 10.17–10.19, 10.28, 10.29,
 18.9–18.11
Goldwater, Barry, 2.9
go/no-go tests, 5.8

government jobs, not
 entitlements, 16.11–16.12
government-revenue sharing,
 12.1–12.2
Great Depression, 10.4, 11.7

H
Hoover, Herbert, 2.10, 10.3
House of Representatives
 constitutional role of,
  6.1–6.2, 6.10
 expulsion of members,
  17.13
 impeachment,
  16.14–16.15, 16.20
 impeachment and, 16.10,
  16.13, 16.17, 16.23, 17.15
 republican Constitution
  Party and, 18.17–18.18
Humphrey, Hubert, 2.7
hybrid rulemaking, 6.6

I
impeachment and conviction
 failure of congressmen to
  use, 16.1–16.2
 limiting losses and,
  16.4–16.9
 offsetting powers and,
  16.6–16.9
 preventing losses and,
  16.2–16.3, 16.7,
  16.9–16.22, 16.24
 Progressives and,
  16.23–16.24
 sole power residing
  with Congress, 3.8,
  17.14–17.15
 use of, 16.10–16.16
 zero tolerance
  for defying the

Index

Constitution and, 16.16–16.22
inflation
  common stock and, 10.23
  government-issued paper money and, 10.2, 10.6–10.10, 10.13–10.14, 10.16–10.17, 10.21, 10.28
  paper money and, 10.2
  unnaturally-low interest rates and, 10.6
informal rulemaking, 6.6
interest rates
  government intervention and, 10.6–10.11, 10.13
  natural levels of, 10.5, 10.9
Intolerable Acts (1774), 2.4
Iraq War, 15.8
IRS, misconduct by, 16.22

J
Jackson, Andrew, 10.2, 18.3
Jefferson, Thomas, 18.2
Johnson & Johnson, response to Tylenol murders, 7.5
judicial branch
  agencies and, 17.10–17.11
  impeachment and, 16.17, 16.19
  judicial power vested in courts, not agencies, 17.10–17.11
  laws directing, 5.1, 5.6–5.9
  offsetting powers and, 16.6–16.9
  Progressive dominance and, 17.16
  scope of powers, 3.7–3.8, 3.12–3.14
  terms of employment governed by Constitution, 17.13

L
Larson, Edward, 2.4
legislative branch
  agencies and, 17.8–17.11
  delegation of powers, unconstitutional, 6.1–6.10
  impeachment and, 16.17
  laws directing executive and judicial branches, 5.1–5.9
  offsetting powers and, 16.6–16.9
  Progressive dominance and, 17.16
  scope of powers, 3.3–3.8, 3.12–3.15, 17.8–17.11
  terms of employment governed by Constitution, 17.13
  unreadable laws and, 4.1, 4.4, 4.7–4.10, 4.12–4.13
Lincoln, Abraham, 18.6
lossy money stock, 10.10–10.16

M
Madison, James, 1.9, 2.4, 2.6
managers, economic efficiency and, 12.15
Mason, George, 2.3–2.4, 5.4–5.5
Mayo Clinic, 7.5
media and advertising, abortion and, 9.12–9.13
military action

I.7

congressional oversight of presidents as Constitution defiance, 17.1–17.6
forward basing, 15.4–15.6
government scope and, 3.3–3.4
moral war and, 11.11–11.14, 11.17, 17.2
moral war as following the Constitution, 15.1–15.4
more- vs. less-free nations and, 11.4–11.7
parties failing to secure from war, 18.9–18.10
peacemaking boundaries in the Constitution and, 11.1, 11.14–11.24
resistance and strength and, 11.1–11.4, 11.8, 11.22–11.24, 18.11
rules of engagement and, 3.3
scope of government and, 8.4
unilateral action and, 14.9, 17.4–17.5
militia, Constitution and, 11.15
misleading laws, 7.1–7.14
moral war, 15.1–15.4, 15.8–15.12, 17.2. *see also* military action
Morris, Gouverneur, 1.9
Mortgage Bankers Association, 1.6
Murphy, Christopher, 14.18, 16.19

N
National Resources Defense Council, 6.3–6.4
National Socialist German Workers' Party (Nazis), 11.7, 11.10
NATO, 15.1–15.12
Necessary and Proper Clause, 8.6
negotiated rulemaking, 6.7
new party design, 18.14–18.19
NFIP, 18.13
notice-and-comment rulemaking, 6.6

O
oaths or affirmations, 17.11–17.13
Obama, Barack, 18.19

P
Panic of 1893, 18.6–18.7
Panic of 1896, 18.6–18.8
paper money, 10.1, 10.2, 10.12, 10.17–10.18, 18.2–18.3, 18.7, 18.9, 18.11–18.14
peace through resistance, economic strength, 11.8–11.10
pharmaceutical drugs, small government and, 7.1–7.6, 7.12–7.14
presidents
  abortion and, 9.1
  agencies and, 17.16
  appointment of administrators not following the Constitution and, 16.1–16.2

Index

appointment of judges not following the Constitution and, 16.1
block grants and, 12.1–12.4
congressional oversight regarding war and, 17.1–17.2, 17.6
delegation of powers, unconstitutional, 6.9–6.10
executive power vested in, 13.7, 17.9–17.10
failure to follow Constitution regarding war, 11.1
impeachment and, 16.10–16.11
laws directing executive and judicial branches, 5.1–5.6
oath or affirmation and, 17.11–17.13
removing people from government positions, 17.13–17.14
republican Constitution Party and, 18.17
role in lawmaking, 13.4
scope of powers, 3.7–3.11, 3.13
treaties and, 14.1, 14.3–14.5, 14.13, 14.17–14.18
unreadable laws and, 4.1–4.4, 4.7–4.10, 4.12
productive money stock, 10.20–10.30
Progressive Era, 1.10
Progressives, 2.10, 9.22–9.23, 9.29–9.30, 11.7, 13.8, 16.19, 16.23–16.24, 17.8, 17.15–17.17
property rights
pharmaceutical drug development and, 7.1, 7.6, 7.8–7.9, 7.12–7.14
value of money and, 10.16, 10.28–10.30, 18.4–18.5, 18.9–18.11

R

Reagan, Ronald, 1.3, 2.1, 2.7–2.9, 18.18
religious faith, abortion and, 9.10–9.11
republican Constitution Party, 18.14–18.19
Republican Party
current, 18.5–18.8
first, 18.1–18.3, 18.8
Revolutionary War, 2.3, 2.6, 16.18
Roosevelt, Franklin, 2.7, 10.3–10.4
"rulemaking" powers, administrative bureaus, 3.9–3.10
rules of engagement, 3.3, 11.15–11.20, 17.3–17.5

S

Sallie Mae, 18.13
Schoenbrod, David, 6.3–6.4
scope, government
basics of, 3.2–3.15
block grants and, 12.3–12.6, 12.14–12.15
government brought into alignment with Constitution, 18.10
laws that exceed, 8.1–8.8

I.9

nature of government
    work and, 14.6
  political, commercial,
    and support scope,
    8.4–8.5
  property rights and,
    7.12–7.13
  state governments and,
    4.9
  treaties and, 3.3–3.5,
    14.2–14.3
Senate
  appointment of judges
    not following the
    Constitution and, 16.1
  constitutional role of,
    6.1–6.2, 6.10
  expulsion of members,
    17.13
  filibuster/cloture,
    13.1–13.9
  impeachment and,
    16.10, 16.13, 16.15,
    16.17, 16.19, 16.23,
    17.15
  republican Constitution
    Party and, 18.17–18.18
  scope of powers, 3.2–3.11
  simple-majority voting
    and, 13.1–13.4
  treaties and, 14.1,
    14.3–14.5, 14.13,
    14.17–14.19
shopping, adding value
  through. *also see* customers,
  adding value, 17.7–17.8
simple-majority voting,
  13.1–13.9, 14.13, 16.20
slavery, failure to use
  constitutional powers to
  end, 9.16–9.19, 9.21

Soviet Union. *see* Union of
  Soviet Socialist Republics
  (USSR)
state caucuses, new party
  design and, 18.17–18.18
states
  abortion and, 9.1–9.2,
    9.19–9.21, 9.23–9.26,
    9.27–9.30
  chartering banks,
    10.2–10.3
  coercion by state-
    government people,
    12.10–12.12
  congressional oversight
    and, 17.1
  executive power of, 3.10
  national government
    spending on, 12.1–
    12.6, 12.9–12.16
  powers delegated by the
    people, 17.11
  scope of powers,
    3.10–3.11
stealth tax, government
  manipulation of interest
  rates, 10.13–10.15
supermajority voting, 13.5
Supreme Court *see also*
  judicial branch
  abortion and, 9.23–9.25,
    16.20–16.21
  judicial power vested in,
    17.10–17.11

T
tariffs, 14.9–14.11, 17.3–17.5,
  18.7
taxes
  in Colonial America, 1.9,
    8.7

Index

income tax, 3.11
national government spending on states and, 12.4–12.6
proportional taxation, 3.11
Revolutionary War and, 16.18
stealth tax, government manipulation of interest rates, 10.13–10.15
thalidomide, 7.8–7.9
Thune, John, 14.18
tort-case standard, 16.14
Townshend Acts (1767), 2.3–2.4
treaties
    constitutional treatymaking, 14.17–14.19
    effective, 14.13–14.17, 17.4–17.5
    government scope and, 3.3–3.4, 14.2–14.3
    as laws, 14.1–14.2
    presidents and, 14.3–14.5
    unilateral action vs., 14.5–14.13, 14.19
    war treaties, 15.1–15.4, 15.8–15.12
    war treaties not following the Constitution, 15.6–15.10
Truman, Harry, 2.7
Tylenol Murders (1982), 7.5

U

unilateral action, 14.5–14.13, 14.19, 17.4–17.5

Union of Soviet Socialist Republics (USSR), 11.5–11.6, 11.9–11.10, 11.13
unions, Ronald Reagan and, 2.7–2.8
unreadable laws, 4.1–4.14

V

Van Buren, Martin, 10.2–10.4, 10.10, 10.12, 18.3
Van Hollen, Chris, 14.18, 16.19
vice president
    impeachment and, 16.10, 16.23
    scope of powers, 3.7–3.8, 3.11, 3.14
    simple-majority voting and, 13.3–13.4
    terms of employment governed by Constitution, 17.13–17.14
voting age, 3.12

W

war. *see* military action
War of 1812, 18.2
Washington, George, 1.3, 2.1–2.6
working, adding value through, 17.7–17.8
World War II, 11.4–11.7, 11.9–11.10, 14.16

www.ingramcontent.com/pod-product-compliance
Lightning Source LLC
Chambersburg PA
CBHW051524020426
42333CB00016B/1764